From Walras to Pareto

European Heritage in Economics and the Social Sciences

Edited by: Jürgen G. Backhaus
University of Erfurt

Frank H. Stephen
University of Strathclyde

Volume 1
Joseph Alois Schumpeter
Jürgen G. Backhaus

Volume 2
The Soul of the German Historical School: Methodological Essays on Schmoller, Weber, and Schumpeter
Yuichi Shionoya

Volume 3
Friedrich Nietzsche (1844-1900): Economy and Society
Jürgen G. Backhaus and Wolfgang Drechsler

Volume 4
From Walras to Pareto
Jürgen G. Backhaus and J. A. Hans Maks

From Walras to Pareto

edited by

Jürgen G. Backhaus
University of Erfurt, Germany

J. A. Hans Maks
Maastricht University, The Netherlands

Springer

Library of Congress Control Number: 2006923764

ISBN:10: 0-387-33756-3 (Printed on acid-free paper) e-ISBN-10: 0-387-33757-1
ISBN-13: 978-0387-33756-2 e-ISBN-13: 978-0387-33757-9

Printed in the United States of America.

9 8 7 6 5 4 3 2 1

springer.com

Table of Contents

Contributors

From Walras to Pareto

Prof. Dr. Dr. h.c. Jürgen G. Backhaus Lic. jur.

Prof. Dr. Jan van Daal

Prof. Dr. Roland Dillmann†

Prof. Dr. Hans Frambach

Assoc. Prof. Yukihiro Ikeda

Dr. Albert Jolink

Prof. Dr. J. A. Hans Maks

Dr. Michael McLure

Prof. Kayoko Misaki

PD Dr. Dr. Helge Peukert

1. From Walras to Pareto. Introduction

Jürgen Backhaus and Hans Maks

One may have various reasons for a volume of papers devoted to and inspired by Walras and Pareto. Pareto succeeded Walras in 1893 on the chair of Political Economy at the University of Lausanne. The relation between the two was not always without tensions, although Pareto, on the occasion of his 25 years jubilee celebration, at least in part, transferred the honours offered to him to Walras. Indeed, one may say that to a substantial extent important parts of the works of Pareto would not have been possible without the insights of Walras.

Both eminent scientists also have in common that the image of their inheritance professed to the common university trained economic scholars ('cutes') is a highly restricted caricature of the fullness of their essential insights and contributions, whereas students of sociology or politicology may even finish their academic studies without ever having heard the name of Pareto.

What 'cutes' "know" about Walras amounts to the following caricature. Walras developed the general economic equilibrium model, but did not care about uniqueness and stability of an equilibrium. It is a model with exchange and production only and it assumes an auctioneer who announces price vectors to establish the equilibrium. The model presupposes perfect information and is static and certainly not dynamic. Walras had a bias towards free competition and laisser faire and neglected monopoly and taxation.

Pareto is known by the 'cutes' as the founding father of welfare economics. At best one is informed about the notions of Pareto-optimality conditions and the first and second welfare theorems. But welfare economics is in general disappearing from the university research and teaching programs, replaced as it is by consumer and producer surpluses in the nowadays flourishing partial industrial economics programs.

To a certain extent these developments did provoke correcting reactions. One might refer for Walras to the impressive volumes edited by Donald Walker (2002) and to *e.g.* Maks and Van Daal (2007). Regarding Pareto one may mention *e.g.* the works of Tarascio (1968), Samuels (1974), Backhaus (1978), and McLure (2001). The present volume might contribute in this respect but it also shows that even nowadays the heritage of Walras and Pareto inspires to reflection, to new interpretations and, perhaps, to new caricatures, yet it might also reveal hitherto neglected aspects or applications.

Jan van Daal's essay "Léon Walras's Economics: From Pure to Normative?" discusses certain aspects of the above sketched caricature of Walras. He explains that the guiding principle for the work of Walras was his desire to contribute to the solution of the Social Question, dealing with the fact that so many people are living in misery. He sketches Walras's vision on the social sciences and indicates how economics fits in this vision. Van Daal also reveals Walras's insights on applied monetary economics, *i.e.* how one should attempt to stabilise the cyclical fluctuations of an economy. In this context he emphasises the various steps towards reality Walras made in extending the scope of his equilibrium model with capital, fiat money and commodity based money. He concludes that the quantity theory of money does not hold in this pure extended equilibrium model.

The essence of Walras's pure theory is contained in the five editions of the Éléments and the two Études. Walras aims at analysing a consecutive sequence, not without dynamic elements, of temporary equilibria from period to period. Furthermore, 'intra-period' analysis, concerning the agents' behaviour during a certain period, was dynamic in the first three editions of the Éléments in the sense that Walras was trying to describe how the groping processes to the period's equilibrium take place. The ban on 'out of equilibrium production' is just introduced in the fourth edition probably because Walras became aware of the complexity of the analysis of groping while allowing disequilibrium production.

The normative part of Walras's work, as Van Daal concludes, is mainly to be found in his *Études d'économie sociale* and *Études d'économie politique appliquée*. In these two books he rather dealt with monopoly and other market organizations than free competition and focused also on taxation, public goods and state ownership of land.

The contribution "The General Equilibrium Theory in Japanese Economic Thought: From Walras to Morishima" of Kayoko Misaki is a very informative review of the development of the reception and diffusion of the various schools of economics among the Japanese scientists with a special emphasis on the influence of Walras.

An important Japanese economist in his days was Fukuda (1874-1930). He was a professor at the Tokyo University of Commerce. This university was not aiming, as the 'imperial' University of Tokyo was, at educating future government officials. By consequence there was more scope for heterodox (including Walrasian) economics. Among Fukuda's students were Tezuka and Nakayama. Tezuka translated and published a substantial part of the Éléments as early as 1933 in Japanese, twenty-one years before the famous Jaffé translation into English.

Nakayama was also influenced by Schumpeter, one of the first economists who appreciated Walras in his full non-caricatural extent. Nakayama published a book in 1933 under the title *Pure Economics*. This book became an influential bestseller, probably because it explained the general equilibrium theory in non-mathematical terms.

Although at the University of Tokyo the Walrasian influence was not substantial, it produced one of the most important Japanese Walrasian economists, namely Takuma Yasui. Yasui became well known after the Second World War for his contribution to the stability conditions of the Walrasian model.

Further, of course, Michio Morishima is mentioned, a graduate and former professor of the Kyoto University, the place to be for sociology. Morishima's lifetime task exists of three projects. The study of general equilibrium theory, the synthesis of economics and sociology, and the study of Ricardo, Marx and Walras. Walras was in favour of the nationalisation of land because of his insight that in a progressive economy the wages would remain on rather low levels. Among other things, Morishima reproaches Walras for not having developed the pure economics that would found his social economics.

One of the avenues that might lead to this connection of Walras's pure economics and his social economics is suggested in the essay "Gross Substitutes, Walras's Rareté and the Stability of the Middle Class" by J.A. Hans Maks. He starts with the observation that Walras is very much aware of the uniqueness and stability problem. This is argued with quotations from the Éléments. Nevertheless it is also clear that the assumptions of Walras were not sufficient to guarantee stability of the groping process.

Maks, however, proposes to analyse in what way Walras's theory, retaining the simple cardinal, strongly additive utility concept he uses, should be supplemented to obtain stability. In the end it turns out that the income distribution should not be too unequal. The more middle class agents there are in an economy, the less likely it is that in the aggregate gross substitutability does not hold. Agents with low incomes, close to existence minimum levels, as well agents with very high levels of income, in the neighbourhood of bliss, destabilise the groping process.

One might relate this finding to the value of 'alfa' in Pareto's well-known income distribution function. It might even be possible to indicate a set of values of 'alfa' that generate stability. On the one hand, Maks's result grounds Walras's point of view that land should be nationalised, since nationalisation leads probably to a more equal income distribution. However, it is also obvious that other means to arrange a stability feasible income distribution are also acceptable.

As observed above partial industrial economics is flourishing. If econometrics is applied in the context of the functioning of markets it is in most cases in industrial economics. Up till this moment it proves to be hardly possible to directly estimate a model for a substantial part of the economy, with all its interrelated details, that resembles closely enough the conditions of free competition. The reason behind this is, among others, the lack of relevant sufficiently detailed market data. Apart from experimental economics, econometrics uses usually statistical data, that are aggregated such that they are hardly suitable to be applied in the context of an intertemporal general (dis)equilibrium model. So it comes not quite as a surprise that in his contribution "What Went Wrong With Walras" Albert Jolink observed that the leading econometricians of the thirties of the last century felt more sympathy for Cournot's analyses. Nobel Prize winner Jan Tinbergen, for instance, was of the opinion that Walras's model of free competition is not acceptable "in every case, which is increasingly important for the economy, as the amount of monopolies and half-monopolies grows due to the increasing concentration". Here one might be inclined to add that Walras would agree with Tinbergen not to apply his pure model of free competition in cases where reality is not close enough to free competition.

Robert Dillmann and Hans Frambach address in their essay the theme of "Economic Equilibria and the Balancing Act between Total and Partial Analysis". This paper is written from a mathematical point of view rather than an economic standpoint. Sometimes the authors seem to be a little amazed about what they found when reading Walras's *Éléments* and related works. Some bold, but not always new, assertions can therefore be found in their paper. Agreeing with Walras, Pareto, and Schumpeter, the authors signal the shortcomings and dangers of partial analyses as advocated by Cournot and Marshall. They describe the stages of development of Walras's pure theory of free competition, but emphasise his opinion that equilibrium is an ideal and not a real state, a state towards which things tend under a régime of free competition. A state that will never be reached because everything that is assumed constant in the beginning of the equilibrating process will change and the process will start all over again.

Dillmann and Frambach mention that the mathematical theory of fixed points has solved Walras's problems concerning the existence of equilibrium. Further they deal with stability and uniqueness problems. They agree with Walras that for simplicity reasons it is better to use constant technical coefficients in his pure theory, but at the same time they reproach him that he only developed a theory of economic progress and did not rigorously deal with technological progress, as Schumpeter did. This leads the authors to the conclusion that Walras's theory on free competition might be less suitable for competition policy; this conclusion which could have been a little more subtle if they had examined other writings by Walras than his *Éléments* only. All in all, however, it was a fruitful idea to invite trained mathematicians to read Walras and to give their comments. These comments rather grint towards Pareto's approach.

The contribution by Yukihiro Ikeda focuses on "Léon Walras and the English Classical School: Walras's Production Theory Revisited." He emphasises received opinions regarding the diametrically opposing views of the Classical and Marginal Schools. Adam Smith as 'the' icon of the Classical School was one of the first scholars to detect the movement of market prices towards their natural level under sufficiently competitive conditions. Natural levels means in this context prices covering total average costs. Ikeda brings in Walras's assertions in the Éléments that in equilibrium entrepreneurs do not make profits or losses. Hence, he rightfully concludes that in this respect insights of Smith as classical icon and those of Walras as neo-classical 'champion' coincide.

Ikeda moreover focuses also upon the constancy of the technical coefficients Walras assumes within a period. Of course, he is also aware of the fact that Walras defends himself for using this assumption for simplicity reasons. He acknowledges nevertheless this simplification as a striking similarity of Neo-classical and Classical analysis. One might add here that even u-shaped average cost curves or their shift does not necessarily prevent equilibrium prices covering total average costs under suitable conditions.

The essays on Pareto have in common that they take the distinction Pareto introduces between logical and non-logical action of the agents under consideration as their starting point. Pareto, as many of the great economists addressing the philosophy of social sciences issue,[1] relates his definition of the homo agens *c.q.* homo oeconomicus with his philosophy of the social science.[2] Pareto wrestles with what one might nowadays call the distinction between objective rationality, a concept according to which the agent strives after an economic goal and also knows the means to achieve it, and subjective or bounded rationality according to which the action goals may be of whatever nature and the acting agent may not precisely 'objectively' know the means to achieve his ends. To make a similar distinction Pareto introduced logical versus non-logical action.

Logical or rational behaviour may be directed at objective or subjective ends but the means *c.q.* actions are effective. And this is true for the agent also after the action: no regrets and no reflective expectations that another action would have been better. In this context one may distinguish between a homo oeconomicus, a homo ethicus, a homo religious etc, as long as they are effective in whatever end they strive after. And to be more precise: the homo oeconomicus may go for maximum wealth (an objective goal) or for maximum (ordinal) utility (a subjective goal).

Non-logical (or subjective or bounded rational) behaviour is aiming at objective or subjective goals but the aimed action is not per se effective in the sense that the agent is fully informed about the consequences of his action. He may be disappointed afterwards, caused by changes in his preferences or by unforeseen external changes. The latter may in its turn induce changes in preferences. According to Pareto both types of action need dedicated explanation in the positive social sciences, as long as the efficacy of the means is verifiable.

The theories of non-logical actions should explain the forces behind preferences and, hence, the changes or even the instability in those preferences. Economics should study not only logical behaviour but also non-logical conduct. Moreover economics should be part of a multidisciplinary social science that combines all the information we have on ethics, economics, politics etc.[3]

In the essay "Vilfredo Pareto and Public Choice" Helge Peukert elaborates on Pareto's non-logical conduct analysis. Pareto distinguishes as forces behind tastes and preferences residues (or sentiments), pseudo-logical justifications build upon these sentiments, denoted as derivations, and interests. Interests are the analysed forces of received public economics.

Peukert sketches the six classes of residues Pareto distinguishes. Changes in residues may in their turn be influenced by the logical factor: logical actions and interests. Logical and non-logical-actions are hence equally important for Pareto. Peukert concludes that many of Pareto's residues may be not so functional today, but we should not forget to see his theory of residues as tentative and further research may "enlarge or reduce Pareto's classification".

In "Two Views on Pareto's Current Relevance: Warren Samuel's Foreword to Pareto, Economics and Society" Michael McLure reacts on Samuel's foreword to his book. The main issue between the two is the question whether Pareto's general political sociology tends to an equilibrium in society or not. The reconciliation between the two vision proposed by McLure is based upon the distinction between equilibrium within a period and the uncoordinated, not foreseen sequence of period equilibria or the path of social change as it might be caused by non-logical actions.

Acceptation of this solution may open opportunities to integrate political sociology with economics. However, one cannot help to be inclined to agree with McLure as being not overoptimistic in this respect. "Orthodox" economics still does not fully appreciate the essence of Walras's pure theory in aiming at a usually uncoordinated time path of period equilibria. It remains to a too large extent within the realms of full objective rational behaviour. To this one may add that a similar attitude often holds for political sociologists in their lack of willingness to appreciate the potentials of economic analyses based upon tendencies towards equilibria, even if they are confined to movements towards an equilibrium in a period.

NOTES

1. Like John Stuart Mill in his *"Essays on Some Unsettled Questions of Political Economy"* (1874), Menger in his *"Untersuchungen über die Methode der Sozialwissenschaften und der politischen Ökonomie insbesondere"* (1883), Robbins in his *"An Essay on the Nature and Significance of Economic Science"* (1934) and von Mises in his *"The Ultimate Foundation of Economic Science"* (1958).
2. For a review of the philosophies of social sciences of Mill, Menger, Robbins and Von Mises see Maks in Backhaus (ed.) (2005), 209-222.
3. See Pareto (1980), 166-167.

REFERENCES

Backhaus, J. (1978). "Pareto on Public Choice", *Public Choice*, Vol. 33, No. 1, 5 17, reproduced in John Wood and Michael McLure (eds), *Vilfredo Pareto: Critical Assessments*, 1999, vol. 4, London: Routledge, 395-407.

Fukuoka, M. and Koyama, A. (1959). "Reexamination of the General Equilibrium Theory à la Cassel". (In Japanese) *Kikan Riron Keizaigaku*, 9(1/2).

Maks, J.A.H. and van Daal, J. (2007). "Léon Walras: What Cutes Know and What They Should Know". In Backhaus, J. (ed.), *Founders of Modern Economics*, Cheltenham: Edward Elgar.

Maks, J.A.H. (2005). "Neo-Austrian, Industrial and Ordo-Austrian Competition Policy". In Backhaus, J.G. (ed.), *Modern Applications of Austrian Thought*, London: Routledge, 209-222.

McLure, M. (2001). *Pareto Economics and Society: The Mechanical Analogy*, London: Routledge.

Menger, C. (1883). *Untersuchungen über die Methode der Sozialwissenschaften und der Politischen Ökonomie insbesondere*, Leipzig: Duncker & Humblot.

Mill, J.S. (1974) [1874]. *Essays on some Unsettled Questions of Political Economy*, 2nd edition, reprinted, Clifton, NJ: Kelley.

Nakayama, I. (1933). *Junsuikeizaigaku* (Pure Economics), Tokyo: Iwanamishoten.

Pareto, V. (1980) [1916]. *Compendium of General Sociology*, Abridged with approval of the author by Giulio Farina from Pareto's Trattato di Sociologia Generale, Elisabeth Abbott (ed.), Minneapolis: University of Minnesota Press.

Pareto, V. (1990) [1896]. *Études d'économie sociale* (Théorie de la répartition de la richesse sociale), edited by Pierre Dockès, under the auspices of the Centre Auguste et Léon Walras, Lyon, Vol. IX of Auguste et Léon Walras: Œuvres économiques complètes, Paris: Économica.

Pareto, V. (1992) [1898]. *Études d'économie politique appliquée* (Théorie de la production de la richesse sociale), edited by Jean-Pierre Potier, under the auspices of the Centre Auguste et Léon Walras, Lyon, Vol. X of Auguste et Léon Walras: Œuvres économiques complètes, Paris: Économica.

Robbins, L. (1948). *An Essay on the Nature and Significance of Economic Science*, 2nd ed., revised and extended, London: Macmillan.

Samuels, W.J. (1974). *Pareto on Policy*, Amsterdam: Elsevier Scientific Publishing Company.

Tarascio, V.J. (1968). *Pareto's Methodological Approach to Economics*, Chapel Hill: University of North Carolina Press.

Walker, D.A. (ed.) (2002). *The Legacy of Léon Walras*, Cheltenham (UK): Edward Elgar Publishing Ltd.

Von Mises, L. (1962). *The Ultimate Foundation of Economic Science: An Essay on Method.* Princeton, NJ: Nostrand.

PART I

Léon Walras

2. The General Equilibrium Theory in Japanese Economic Thought: From Walras to Morishima

Kayoko Misaki

Shiga University, Japan

Abstract

The aim of this paper is to show how Japanese economists understood the political and ideological implications of Walras's general equilibrium theory in its diffusion process. It was in the 1930s that Japanese economists began to work on the general equilibrium theory. Although close surveys of their theoretical contributions have already been made, little attention has been given to its political and ideological aspects. In this paper, therefore, I would like to focus attention on these arguments that have been ignored and try to show the possibilities of general equilibrium theory as social science.

Keywords: General Equilibrium Theory, Walras, Japanese Economic Thought

JEL classification: A12, B13

1. ESTABLISHMENT OF 'MODERN ECONOMICS' IN JAPAN

Let us begin by focusing attention on the definition of 'Kindai Keizaigaku' (modern economics) in Japan, as it goes to the very heart of the problem. In Japan, the term 'modern economics' has been generally used to indicate non-Marxian economics after the marginal revolution. The emphasis is always put on non-Marxian. It also excludes the historical school and institutional economics. Thus the term 'modern' is not necessarily used in relation to periodization.[1]

This is probably a good illustration of how modern economics was established in Japan in the 1930s in opposition to other economics, especially to Marxian economics. At that time, it was Walras's general equilibrium theory that came to the mainstream of modern economics, although other marginalist theories such as those of Marshall and Jevons had already been introduced.

In the process of its modernization after the Meiji Restoration of 1867, Japan first introduced British classical economics as a propaganda of liberalism. They believed that it would serve to eliminate feudalistic ideas of the Tokugawa Period (1600-1867) and to diffuse such modern notions as freedom and independence.[2]

In 1889, the Constitution of the Empire of Japan, which was based on the German model, was established. The Japanese government decided to formulate basic policies of industrialization, following the example of Germany's vigorous progress of those days. The government diffused the German social policy school, which soon dominated the mainstream instead of the British classical school.

Marxian Economics was introduced at the beginning of the 1900s and diffused as anti-propaganda to the militaristic policy (the Sino-Japanese War of 1894-95 and the Russo-Japanese War of 1904-05) of the government and to the reactionary elements of the Japanese social policy school. The influence of Marxism became so strong especially after the Russian Revolution as to attract most of the liberal intellectuals and the economists who were concerned with the recession and impoverishment of rural communities in those days.

The predominance of Marxian economics, however, did not last. It was forbidden by a state law when the Mukden Incident broke out in 1931. During the war, Japan had to seek an alternative economic theory, as the social policy school had already broken up because of internal divisions.

In those days, under the influence of the extreme right, 'Seiji Keizaigaku' (political economy) that was based on the German economics of F. v. Gottl-Ottlilienfeld was prevailing to justify the controlled economy. On the other hand, a few economists came to pay attention to the international development of general equilibrium theory. The London School established the Econometric Society in 1930 and *Econometrica* in 1933. The Austrian School strengthened its tendency towards general equilibrium theory, starting the *Zeitschrift für Nationalökonomie*, where English-speaking economists also began to contribute.

In Japan, on the contrary, '*modern economics was like a small floating island in the sea of Marxism*' (Yasui, 1980, p. 250) although marginal economic theory had already been fragmentally introduced. Those Japanese economists that were establishing 'modern economics' were the minority and were confronted with the invisible dominance of Marxian economics and with the popularization of rightist economics that served Japanese militarism in the 1930s.

It was in this situation that Juro Tedzuka (1896-1943) published the first Japanese translation of Walras's *Eléments.*[3] In 1933, he published its first volume that contains only the theories of exchange and production. He failed to publish a second one because of the war although he had already completed it. It was after his death in 1954 that both volumes were published.

In the first volume, Tedzuka introduced Walras's life briefly but did not mention his socialist thinking or his idea of nationalization of land. In the preface, Tedzuka referred to G. Sensini's remark in *La teoria della rendita* (1912): "Unfortunately Walras abandoned his study of pure economics and proceeded to that of utopian applied economics moved by his nature as social reformer."

Tedzuka maintained that Walras's true contribution should be found in his recognition of the interdependency of economic phenomena whether he had been conscious of it or not. Pareto developed Walras's general equilibrium theory by discarding the concept of cardinal number that had remained in his marginal utility theory. Tedzuka says:

> Today, there exists neither subjective theory of value nor labor theory of value, for the disinterested economists. The only theory that exists is general equilibrium theory. Those who aim at a disinterested inquiry of the economic phenomenon must begin with Walras and with Pareto.

What we notice here is that Tedzuka emphasized the disinterested character of general equilibrium theory. However it does not necessarily follow that he was not interested in ideological arguments. On the contrary, it is obvious that he had a great detailed knowledge of the history of ideas in France. The 6624 books on French economics, philosophy and socialism of which he made a collection during his stay in France (1920-1926) is well known as the Tedzuka Library of Otaru University of Commerce. His real intention was to present a more universal point of view against the contemporary economists who were insisting on the particularity of the Japanese economy.

On the other hand, during the war, the school of political economy countered him on the pretense that pure economics could pursue nothing concrete, nothing Japanese but something universal. Tedzuka replied that such was the characteristic of pure economics, as it aimed to be a positive science. Thus modern economics in Japan was given a neutral and non-ideological characteristic at its beginning.

2. TOKUZO FUKUDA (1874-1930) AND HIS DISCIPLES: THE GOLDEN AGE OF HITOTSUBASHI

In the 1930s, those who diffused Walras's general equilibrium theory in Japan were not in the mainstream.

In this section, we will look more carefully into their academic background. An important point to note is that most of them were under the influence of Tokuzo Fukuda (1874-1930). He was not only a great economist but also a great educator who trained many pioneers of modern economics in Japan.

Fukuda had an opportunity to study economics in Germany from 1898 to 1901. He was influenced by Lujo Brentano and received a doctorate at the University of Munich.[4] After returning to Japan, he took an active part in the diffusion of the social policy school that was dominating the main stream of Japanese economics in those days. However, he was not satisfied with orthodox economics, and his interest shifted to Marshall, Marx and Pigou. In the end, he was strongly opposed to Marxian economics and advocated welfare economics of the Cambridge school.

Fukuda set his disciples the task of translating the literature on marginal theory into Japanese. Under his encouragement, Shinzo Koizumi published the translation of Jevons (1913),[5] Juro Tedzuka published the translations of Gossen (1920) and of Walras (1933), Kinnosuke Otsuka translated Marshall (1924-25) and Ichiro Nakayama published the translation of Cournot (1936). Though Fukuda himself was not good at mathematics, he realized the importance of mathematical economics and particularly of Walras's economics.

He taught these disciples except for Koizumi at Hitotsubashi University. It is noteworthy that Hitotsubashi produced many pioneers of modern economics and played an important role in the diffusion process of Walrasian economics in Japan. The time when Fukuda taught these disciples is called 'the Golden Age of Hitotsubashi'.

Let us look briefly at the history of the education of economics in Japan after the Meiji Restoration of 1867. The government established the Imperial University of Tokyo (the predecessor of the present University of Tokyo) in 1877 and then Imperial University of Kyoto (the predecessor of the present University of Kyoto) in 1897. At first, in both of them, economics was taught at the faculty of Law. It was in 1919 that they created a faculty of economics. At the Imperial University of Tokyo, the first dean of the faculty of economics was Noburu Kanai (1865-1933). He was the introducer of the German policy and historical school in Japan and was the president of the Japanese Association for the Study of Social Policy, which was the only economic association in Japan at that time.

When Fukuda was appointed to a professorship at Hitotsubashi, his alma mater in 1919, it was called the Tokyo Higher Commercial School. It was raised to University status in 1920 as the Tokyo University of Commerce. While the faculties of economics at imperial universities were established generally for the purpose of producing government officials, Hitotsubashi was intended for educating businessmen. Its atmosphere has been anti-government, anti-University of Tokyo, independent and liberal. This is also reflected in its education. At Hitotsubashi, not only the orthodox economics but also the other heterodoxies were taught. Its neighboring sciences such as philosophy, mathematics and sociology were also regarded as important. In this sense, Hitotsubashi could play an important role in the education of modern economics.

At Hitotsubashi in 1927, two different types of 'principles of economics' were lectured on. One was on modern economics by Fukuda. The other was on Marxian economics by his disciple Otsuka.

2.1. Kinnosuke Otsuka (1892-1977): From Mathematical Economics to Marxism

Otsuka joined Fukuda's seminar in 1914. At first his major was mathematical economics. In 1919, he went to Columbia University to study it under the direction of Moore. In 1920, after attending some lectures by Webb at LSE, he moved to the University of Berlin. He visited Lausanne in 1922 for about one month to collect documents of Walras and began a correspondence with his daughter Aline Walras. Although he intended to introduce Walras's economics into Japan at first,[6] his interest shifted to Marxism and socialism. When he returned to Japan in 1924 after hearing about the Great Earthquake of 1923, he was a real Marxist.

The documents that he collected in Lausanne are preserved in the library of Hitotsubashi University.

They contain *Le Travail*, which Walras published with Léon Say from 1866-1868 in their association movements. Otsuka also was very involved when Hitotsubashi University bought the Menger Library in 1923.[7]

2.2. Ichiro Nakayama (1898-1980): The Diffusion of Walras's Pure Economics

Among Fukuda's disciples at Hitotsubashi, Ichiro Nakayama contributed most to the diffusion of Walras's pure economics in the 1930s. It is due to his efforts that general equilibrium theory came to be considered as the main stream of modern economics in Japan although the other marginal theories had already been introduced.

Nakayama entered Hitotsubashi University in 1920 and joined Fukuda's seminar in 1921. Though Nakayama was at first interested in Menger's theory of value, Fukuda advised him to begin with Cournot and gave him the task of summarizing Cournot's idea without mathematics. His first paper was published in 1923 with the title 'Surikeizaigaku niokeru futatunokeiko to sonosogono kokoromi tonioite (On the two tendencies in mathematical economics and the attempts to synthesize them)'. In this paper, he dealt with Cournot's quantitative approach to the economic phenomena and Gossen's individualistic and psychological approach to their fundamental cause. He considered Walras's theory as their synthesis and rated it highly. This was one of the earliest papers on Walras in Japan and it didn't receive much attention.

In 1927, Nakayama went to the University of Bonn and studied under the direction of Schumpeter. According to Nakayama, he learned two things from

Schumpeter. One was how to develop Walras's general equilibrium theory without mathematics. He had had no opportunity to read *Das Wesen und der Haupinhalt der theoretischen Nationalökonomie* (1908) or *Theorie der wirtschaftlichen Entwicklung* (1912) until he went to Germany. The other was the attitude towards Marxism. Although Nakayama had intended to study Marx, Fukuda prohibited him from reading books on Marxism and encouraged him to study mathematical economics. Nakayama attended Schumpeter's lectures on the history of economic thought where he criticized Marx directly and indirectly. For Nakayama, it was his first time to study Marx. Under the influence of Schumpeter, Nakayama learned how to oppose modern economics to Marxism.

It is obvious that Nakayama was also affected by Schumpeter's attitude towards Walras's applied and social economics. Nakayama ignored them and devoted himself to Walras's pure economics.

Nakayama returned to Japan in 1929 and published a book on Walras with the title *Junsuikeizaigaku* (Pure economics) in 1933, which became a best-selling book in the field of economic theory. In this book, he maintains that there generally exists interdependency of all the economic phenomena and that general equilibrium theory is a means of grasping it. The aim of pure economics is to understand economic phenomena by applying general equilibrium theory to them.

Nakayama explains that he wrote it under the influence of Schumpeter's *Wesen*. He deals with mathematics only in 14 pages of appendix in his book of 255 pages. It contributed to the diffusion of Walras's equilibrium theory without mathematics in Japan. Nakayama believed that it was due to Schumpeter.

Nakayama took a critical attitude toward the contemporary rightist economists because he couldn't expect any development or progress in its theory. He believed that economic theory should be able to tackle and solve concrete problems in the context of the historical situation of the national economy. This belief is much influenced not only by Schumpeter but also by Fukuda.

Fukuda's other disciple Sugimoto also maintained this belief all his life from the opposite point of view.

2.3. Eiichi Sugimoto (1901-1952): The Critic of the Lausanne School

Fukuda always warned his disciples not to overestimate the validity of pure economic theory while he encouraged them to study mathematical economics. This attitude influenced Sugimoto, one of his disciples, who continued to criticize general equilibrium theory all through his life.

Sugimoto read Marx's *Das Kapital* in Fukuda's seminar in 1922, and studied Marxian crisis theory at first. Fukuda rated Sugimoto's work and personality highly although he was anti-Marxist himself. Fukuda made all possible efforts so that Sugimoto could become an associate professor of Hitotsubashi University in 1929 and that he could go abroad on a scholarship of the Ministry of Education.

From 1929 to 1932, Sugimoto had opportunities to study in Berlin, Kiel, Frankfurt and New York. At the University of Berlin he learned about the business cycle theory from Ernst Wageman and materialism and Marxism from Karl Korsch. He also associated with Leontief there. Under their influences, Sugimoto came to think highly of Econometrics as a means of grasping empirical laws of the economy. In the turmoil of the 1930s, he believed that Econometrics could be a science that could be free from ideology. Sugimoto is known as one of the pioneers of Econometrics in Japan, who derived the demand curve of rice in 1935. However more noteworthy is his critical comment on the Lausanne school. He asserted that general equilibrium theory could not analyze the real economy or the wartime economy of those days and that consequently it permitted the rightist economics to gain power.

In the preface of his *Rironkeizaigaku no Kihonmondai* (The fundamental problems of economic theory) (1939), he claims:

> The economics of the Lausanne school, which recently came to the mainstream of modern economics, considered the economic world basically as general equilibrium of the quantities of all the economic factors and grasped the objective aspect of the economy as self-contained. As the subjective aspect of all the process of economic development has been separated and isolated from the objective one, there will no possibility to unite theory and policy. Perhaps this is the first reason why economic policy is pursued instead of economic theory and why the reconstruction of political economy is being demanded against pure economics. (Sugimoto 1939, pp. 1-2)

On the other hand, Sugimoto criticized the school of 'political economy', which overemphasized the subjective aspect of the economy. He continues:

> However the economic control cannot be done if we ignore the objective situation of economic progress. Indeed, it is possible for us to modify the economic structure, but we should have certain criteria that should be approved from the scientific point of view in order to accomplish this modification. These criteria can be decided and recognized through the analysis of the objective situations. Nevertheless some recent advocates of political economy often jump to the conclusion that they succeeded in making economic theory into policy only by insisting on the predominance of politics over economy or by showing the structure of policies in general. They never take the trouble to show the logic for the objective analysis of the situation. This attitude transforms the principles of economics into a simple politics. It also prevents us from uniting economic theory and policy and brings about the conclusion that doesn't meet the needs of the times in a different sense from that of the Lausanne School. (Ibid., p. 2)

After the Second World War, Sugimoto continued to criticize the Lausanne School and emphasized the validity of Marshall's partial equilibrium theory.

He also insisted on the friendly rivalry between modern economics and Marxian economics,[8] which was not accepted in Japan at that time.

In his *Kindaikeizaigaku no Kaimei* (The explication of modern economics) (1950), which is widely read even now, he gave his own definition of modern economics. It includes all of the economics that were established after the 1860s. Against its usual definition, Marxian economics was also included. He says:

> To exclude Marxian economics from modern economics seems to have certain implications that are related not to science but to party spirit of the united front against the Marxian school. This is just the same as the attitude of Marxian imitators to presume all the non-Marxian economics to be bourgeois economics. Especially in Japan, I am sometimes surprised that the school of pure economics has party spirits although it asserts that science should be free from scientists' vision of the world and rejects Marxian economics as religion. (Sugimoto 1950, Vol. 1, pp. 57-58)

While the contemporary modern economists believed that general equilibrium theory could be free from ideology, Sugimoto pointed out its ideological implications. He explains why many economists support general equilibrium theory although they know that it is irrelevant to the analysis of the real economy. Sugimoto says:

> I think that this is related to the social vision that they have at the bottom of their heart. It is based their economic view that the real economic life will end to equilibrium even today. We cannot help saying that this view comes from the belief that capitalism is a permanent system. ... (Sugimoto 1950, Vol. 1, p. 208)

Sugimoto also attributes the cause of prosperity of pure economics to the backwardness of Japan. According to him, Japanese economists had no idea how to apply economic theory that was imported from a mature capitalistic economy to a Japanese society that still remained feudal in many respects. That is why they tended to consider economic theory as abstract logic rather than as a key to solve real problems of the Japanese economy.

3. TAKUMA YASUI (1909-1995): THE DEVELOPMENT OF GENERAL EQUILIBRIUM THEORY AND ITS METHODOLOGICAL FOUNDATIONS

While modern economics gained force at Hitotsubashi, the University of Tokyo got behind because of the factional dispute between Marxian economists and the others since the foundation of the faculty of economics in 1919. However it produced one of the greatest Walrasian economists in Japan, Takuma Yasui. To quote the phrase (1972) of Takashi Negishi, a former professor of the University of Tokyo, the academic career of Professor Yasui is the history of the development of general equilibrium theory in Japan.

Yasui entered the University of Tokyo in 1928. Before entering the faculty of economics, Yasui was interested in Shakespeare. He read many of his books in the original, which improved his English. It was partly due to his English ability that he could get well acquainted with the stream of economic theory in the world without being influenced by contemporary Japanese economists.

At the University of Tokyo, he first joined the seminar of Eijiro Kawai (1891-1944). Kawai was a liberalistic thinker. The year of 1928 was the turning point for Japanese economists. A mass of communists were arrested and the leading Marxian economists left the University of Tokyo. It caused a bloody affair between students of the left wing and those of the right wing. Kawai criticized both sides. In those days, many of the Japanese liberalists were on the side of Marxists. On the contrary, Kawai was an anti-Marxist though he pursued a study of Marx. In 1939, Kawai was suspended from his job for the censorship of ideas.

Yasui read *On Liberty* by J.S. Mill in Kawai's seminar. Then he worked on Kant and Marx under the influence of Kawai. It was in 1929 that Yasui first became interested in general equilibrium theory. He attended a lecture on Cassel's economic theory by Alfred Amonn who was a visiting professor at the University of Tokyo at that time. Yasui soon found out that the origin of Cassel was Walras. In 1931, he also attended Schumpter's lecture at the University of Tokyo and was influenced by his advice, "Begin with Walras".

In 1933, he began to publish five articles on Walras successively in *the Bulletin of University of Tokyo.*[9] These five articles were epoch-making in the sense that they were almost on the same level as the international studies of general equilibrium theory of those days.

After publishing them in the 1930s, Yasui devoted himself to a study of Hicks and then to that of Slutsuky. He never gave up pursuing his pure economics even under the pressure of the rightist economists during the war. In 1944, Yasui left the University of Tokyo because of the deterioration of research conditions and move to Tohoku University in the northern part of Japan.

After the Second World War, his name became known to the world especially for his contribution to a study of the stability conditions of Walrasian model. As Negishi points out (1972), "his economics was brought up in Japan, and it is a Japanese Economics in a true meaning". Yasui could play an active part in the world although he was never educated or trained abroad.

For Yasui, the aim to study Walras was "to reconsider Walras in the light of development of modern economics, and in another sense, to reconstruct its development on the basis of Walras" (1943). Yasui emphasizes that he had no interest in a study of Walras's economic thought because it didn't mean anything to him. However, contrary to his words, Yasui contributed much to the introduction of Walras's economic thought into Japan. In his essay 'Walras' (1937), he described the details of Walras's life based mostly on his Autobiographia (1900), which Maffeo Pantaleoni published in *Giornale degli Econimisti* in 1908. Yasui mentioned the existence of the more detailed autobiography in Lausanne, which Walras wrote on H.L. Moore's advice.

In the 1930s, Yasui came to be influenced by the school of logical positivism and contributed to its diffusion in Japan. He believed that the method of modern economics should be based on the idea of logical positivism. He denied Marxian economics from this point of view:

> We can disprove its theory of labor value if we consider it as an empirical statement... As long as Marxian economists consider the labor theory of value as an almighty mallet of luck and worship it as an irrefutable proposition, we cannot regard it as empirical science. (Yasui, 1980, p. 256)

In 1952, Yasui was involved in a controversy with Sugimoto on the friendly rivalry between modern economics and Marxian economics. Yasui was pessimistic about it. This controversy ended unexpectedly with the sudden death of Sugimoto in the same year. During this controversy, however, Yasui suggested that modern economists could learn many things from Marxian economics if they were to develop modern economics from a sociological point of view:

> The fact that modern economic theory is not based on the institutional specification of capitalist society does not prevent it from being constructed objectively based on this specification. However, to become well aware of it will be the first step to put theory into effect and in this point, we can adopt many things from Marxian economics. (Yasui, 1979, p. 10)

In 1970, looking back over his academic life, Yasui mentions what modern economics lacks:

> At the beginning of the 1930s, we tackled the problems of tools rather than those of values. We were interested only in finding good tools. After the Second World War, modern economics made such rapid progress that many young economists surpassed us. Modern economics made remarkable progress in tools, but is it all that we need?
>
> When we studied economics, there existed some ideas behind it. In my head, modern economics were, though not clearly, related to my view of science, my thought and my vision of the world. After the war, economics as tools were constructed rapidly. As there was no longer resistance against mathematics, it advanced remarkably at a full speed. Consequently all that could be done was to develop the tools, while the fundamental fact that the character of economics as science is to criticize the society was forgotten. (Ibid., pp. 102-103)

4. MICHIO MORISHIMA (1923-2004): TOWARD A SYNTHESIS OF MODERN ECONOMICS AND OF SOCIOLOGY

In the formation process of modern economics in Japan, Kyoto University played also an important role. Michio Morishima is a graduate and a former professor of the faculty of economics. According to his latest autobiography, *Owariyokereba Subeteyòshi* (All's Well That Ends Well) (2001), he chose Kyoto University in order to learn sociology under Yasuma Takata (1883-1972). Interestingly enough, Morishima first intended to be a sociologist rather than an economist.

Takata was one of the greatest sociologists in Japan. He was also known as one of the greatest modern economists and taught economics at Kyoto University. Before entering the faculty of economics, Morishima had read Takata's *Shakaigakugenri* (The Principle of Sociology) (1919) and *Shakai to Kokka* (Society and State) (1922).

In 1942, Morishima attended Takata's lectures on the principles of economics and on economic philosophy. Takata took over the lecture on economic philosophy by Kozo Ishikawa, who had been arrested because of his ultra nationalistic criticism of the Japanese army in his lectures.

Morishima observes that it was only Takata and his disciple Hideo Aoyama that were teaching authentic economic theory there in those days. The faculty was dominated by the power of the rightists during the war. All the other professors' lectures were prejudiced in favor of the Japanese army. In his lecture on the principles of economics in 1942, Takata read Keynes's *General Theory* (1936), and Hicks's *Capital and Value* (1939). In his lecture on economic philosophy, he taught Weber.

Influenced by those lectures, Morishima started to study Hicks under the direction of Aoyama. Aoyama was not only an economist but also a specialist on Weber. Takata advised Morishima not to study sociology but to devote himself to mathematical economics while he was still young because '*it is the core of social sciences*'.

Morishima says:

> In those days, I had no ability to tell whether his advice was right or wrong. Now I would agree with him. For science should be a rule. To think based on a rule is the minimum requirements for studying. Mathematical economics shows this fact most clearly of all the social sciences. ... I was not an adherent of mathematical economics at first. I may say that I have sought for a chance to get out of mathematical economics after mastering it. (Morishima, 2001, pp. 285-286)

According to Morishima, his lifetime project falls into three parts. The first was a study of general equilibrium theory. The second was a synthesis of economics and of sociology. The third was studies of Ricardo, of Marx and of

Walras. With the intention of connecting the first and the third to the second, he published a book with the title *Sisoutositeno Kindaikeizaigaku* (Modern economics as thought) (1994). As the title shows, this book argues the relationships between modern economics and its thought (vision, values, intention and wish).

The book falls into three parts. In the first part 'Vision and Theory', he deals with Ricardo, Walras, Schumpeter, Hicks, Takata and Wicksell in order to indicate that the flaws in neoclassical price theory. In the second part 'Development of Visions', he argues syntheses of modern economics and of sociology by Marx, Weber, Schumpeter and Pareto. He claims that those syntheses will be the greatest issue among economists in the 21st century. In the third part 'Paradigm change', he criticized von Mises and reconsidered Keynes.

4.1. Was Walras an Evolutionist?

Morishima's purpose to reconsider Walras in this book was to show that Walras could never be an evolutionist although he had a dynamic theory.

In the beginning of the chapter on Walras, Morishima looks back over his argument with Jaffé.[10] Morishima insists that Walras's pure economic theory is supposed to 'observe, describe and explain' an economic society just as the natural sciences and that economist's values have no role in it while social justice is the main issue in social economics.[11] Although Walras supported the nationalization of land, he never argued it in the area of his pure economics. He dealt with it in his social economics.

Morishima quotes the laws of price variations in a progressive economy in Part 7 of *Eléments*.

> Dans une société progressive, le prix du travail, ou le salaire, ne variant pas sensiblement, le prix de la rente, ou le fermage, s'élève sensiblement, et le prix du profit, ou intérêt, s'abaisse sensiblement. (Walras, 1988, p. 597)

Walras intended to present these laws to justify his assertion of nationalization of land. Morishima points out that he conceived them long before he started to write his *Eléments*. As Walras regarded pure economics as a means of studying the social reform, he should have developed a new purc theory that would be suitable for the new economic order. That is to say, there should be interdependence between pure economics and social economics. Pure economics should evolve according to the development of economy. However, Morishima concludes, Walras had no intention of being evolutionist in this sense.

Morishima explains that Walras adopted Say's law like all the other neoclassical economists and that his intention was to save the laws of price variations in a progressive economy.

In the price theory of durable goods, if we consider the equality of all the profit rates to the interest rate, we cannot solve the equations. Under the uniformity of profit rates,[12] if the interest rate is given, the prices of durable goods will be determined in their rental markets. However this price cannot always adjust their demand and supply in general. So Walras adopted the assumption that savings is always equal to investment. In other words, all capital goods can be in demand, no matter how much they may be produced, which Morishima means by Say's law in the sense of microeconomics.[13]

Morishima concludes that Walras failed to evolve his pure theory so that it could fit in with a durable goods economy. Unlike Keynes, he didn't pay attention to its disequilibria. Morishima warns that as it dominates the real economy, the market system will not work. Economists will need to synthesize modern economics and sociology. From this standpoint, Morishima had a high opinion of Pareto and of Schumpeter. He also reevaluates Yasuma Takata's attempt to synthesize general equilibrium theory and sociology.

4.2. Yasuma Takata's Power Theory of Economics

Takata published his five volumes' work *Keizaigaku Shinko* (New Lectures on Economics) from 1929 to 1932, which are known as the first systematic study of general equilibrium theory in Japan. It was also a great success as an advanced textbook in Japan, perhaps comparable to Marshall's *Principles* in the English-speaking world (Sugihara and Tanaka, p. 99). Takata, who was as influenced by Schumpeter as Nakayama was, was always an advocate of general equilibrium theory. However we must not forget that he was a sociologist who pursued his power theory at the same time. He struggled to synthesize general equilibrium theory and his power theory. However he never thought of substituting the latter for the former.

In the preface of Volume 2 of *Keizaigaku Shinko*, he declares that the originality of his book lies not in general equilibrium theory but in the power theory of price. He assumes that a human being is motivated not only by his self-interest but also by his will for power. The latter is remarkable particularly in the market of factors of production. He calls 'power economy' the case where the power of suppliers affects the determination of supply price, while he calls 'pure economy' the case where the price is determined regardless of the social power. He observes that the latter is far from the reality and can be only an assumption. According to Takata, in order to analyze the real economy, we should take the former into consideration.

For example, to Takata, Keynes's explication of involuntary unemployment was insufficient. The downward rigidity of wages should be explained by the social power of working class, and it could happen even under the condition of Say's law. He insists that Walras's general equilibrium is the equilibrium that contains the disequilibrium of labor market.

Morishima points out that Takata's argument in the 1930s is very similar to Hicks's in his *Theory of Economic History* (1969) in the sense that he regarded the labor market as depending on social conditions.

Born in the same year as Keynes and as Schumpeter, Takata wrote more than 100 books and more than 500 articles in his life. Unfortunately so far the study of his theory has been superficial. As Morishima points out, we should explore a further possibility of his theory.[14]

5. CONCLUSION

Walras's general equilibrium theory came to the mainstream of modern economics in the 1930s in Japan. The economists that contributed to its diffusion were the minority, who could escape the strong impact of Marxian economics of the 1920s for some reason or other.

Disregarding Walras's socialist thinking, they insisted that Walras's pure economics was free from the ideology. Their intention was to overcome the invisible predominance of Marxian economics and criticize the right-wing economics that was prevailing in the wartime economy. On the other hand, Sugimoto criticized those modern economists by pointing out the existence of the ideology in general equilibrium theory and related their inclination for generalities to the backwardness of the Japanese economy.

We cannot deny that the intention of Japanese economists for generalities contributed much to the development of Walrasian economic theory. However they have not considered the potentiality of general equilibrium theory as social science.

Morishima gives a warning on this tendency. He concludes that Walras himself failed to build an evolutionary theory of society and reconsiders the attempts of the other economists to synthesize general equilibrium theory and sociology. Especially it's noteworthy that Takata had already tackled this issue in the 1930s in Japan. We should explore a further possibility of Takata's theory as well as throw new light on Walras's economic thought.

NOTES

1. Interestingly enough, this definition of the term was established after the Second World War when Marxian economists were released from jail and returned to the academic world.
2. See Sugihara and Tanaka (1998) for a full account of the relationships between Japanese modernization and economic thought.
3. Strictly speaking, it was not the first introduction of Walras in Japanese. In 1931, Miyoji Hayakawa (1895-1962) published the book with the title Léon Walras Junsuikeizaigaku Nyumon (Introduction to Pure Economics of Léon Walras) that contains the Japanese translation of his Théorie mathématique de la richesse sociale (1883). However this translation is

considered as based on its German version (1881). Born to a wealthy family of a landowner in Hokkaido, Hayakawa had opportunities to study under Dietzel in Bonn and Schumpeter in Vienna from 1921-1925. While many scholars who came from wealthy families turned to socialists at that time, he was interested in mathematical economics. Prior to publications of Tedzuka's translation, he published a detailed biography and bibliography on Walras, which was highly praised by Tedzuka. Hayakawa's article, 'The Application of Pareto's Law of Income to Japanese Data' is known as the first article by a Japanese economist in *Econometrica* (Vol. 19, No. 2, 1951, April). (Matsuda, 1976)

4. His thesis was *Die gesellschaftliche und wirtschaftliche Entwicklung in Japan.* This was published in Stuttgart in 1900 and read widely in the German-speaking world as an excellent introduction to the economic history of Japan. (Sugihara and Tanaka, 1998, p. 60)
5. This is considered as the first introduction of marginal revolution in Japan.
6. For further details, see Nakakubo (2000).
7. On the purchase of the Menger Library by Hitotsubashi University, see Campagnolo (2001).
8. This attitude is also reflected in his good company with Nakayama. From 1937, they taught the two different types of 'principles of economics' in parallel at Hitotsubashi.
9. The first is 'Junsuikeizaigaku to Kakakunoriron – Walras wo chuusintosite (Pure economics and price theory – especially of Walras)' (1933) which is a reconsideration of Walras's marginal productivity theory. The second is 'Kizokuriron to Genkaiseisanryokuriron – Junsuikeizaigaku no nimondai (Theories of imputed value and of marginal productivity – the two problems of pure economics)' (1934). It deals with marginal productivity theory accepting the contemporary idea of cost theory. In the third article 'Jikanyouso to Shihonriron – Walras ni okeru Shizenrishi no gainen (Time elements and capital interest – Walras on natural interest)' (1936), he tries to develop Walras's capital formation theory borrowing the ideas from Boem-Bawerk, Wicksell etc. The fourth (1938) is 'Kahei to Keizaitekikinkou – Walras Kaheiriron no kenkyu (Money and the economic equilibrium – A study of Walras's theory of money). The fifth (1940) is 'Kinkou bunseki to Katei bunseki – Walras Mosakuriron no ichikenkyu (Equilibrium analysis and process analysis – A study of Walras's tatonnement)'. He argued it by borrowing the stable condition from Hicks's *Value and Capital* (1939).
10. Morishima granted that Walras's economics was influenced to some degree by his own quality as social reformer. However, he insists on the other factors that inspired Walras more. One is his poverty and the other was his liking for natural science. According to Morishima, Walras gave up advocating the nationalization of land directly and separated socialism (sociale economics) from science (pure economics) for fear of losing his job that he finally got at the University of Lausanne.
11. Morishima maintains that Walras' method is in this sense the same as Weber's. According to him, Walras adopted perfect competition as the model of pure economics not because he admired laissez-faire, but because he thought it to be the most convenient to analyze the French economy of his time.
12. Hicks didn't assume this in *Value and Capital* (1939).
13. It also means that entrepreneurs are always obedient to the capitalists. See Morishima (1977).
14. On this subject, see also the preface by Morishima in Takata (1995) and Schumpeter and Takata (1998).

REFERENCES

Campagnolo, G. (2001). "The Removal of Carl Menger's Library to Japan in the Aftermath of the First World War and its Impact on Writing the History of his Thought." A paper presented at the Annual Conference of ESHET 22-25, 2001, in Darmstadt.

Hayakawa, M. (1931). *Léon Walras Junsuikeizaigakunyumon* (Introduction to Pure Economics of Léon Walras), Tokyo: Nihonhyoronsha.

Ikeo, A. (1996). "The Advent of Marginalism in Japan." In *Research in the History of Economic Thought and Methodology*, 14, 219-247.

Jaffé, L. (1954). *Léon Walras, Elements of Pure Economics of the Theory of Social Wealth*, London: George Allen & Unwin Ltd.

Matsuda, Y. (1976). "Introduction Professor Hayakawa and Hayakawa Library." In *Catalogue of Hayakawa Library*, Otaru University of Commerce Library, ix-xi.

Morishima, M. (1977). *Walras's Economics: A Pure Theory of Capital and Money*, Cambridge University Press.

Morishima, M. (1994). *Shisoutoshiteno Kindaikeizaigaku* (Modern economics as Thought), Tokyo: Iwanamishoten.

Morishima, M. (2001). *Owariyokereba Subeteyoshi* (All's Well That Ends Well), Tokyo: Asahishinbunsha.

Nakakubo, K. (2000). "A Brief Story to Introduce Walras to Japanese." A paper presented at 2ème colloque de l'Association Internationale Walras, le 22 septembre, 2000, Dijon.

Nakayama, I. (1933). *Junsuikeizaigaku* (Pure Economics), Tokyo: Iwanamishoten.

Negishi, T. (1972). "Yasui Takuma kyoju to Ippankinkouriron no Hatten (Professor Takuma Yasui and the developpment of general equilibrium theory)." In *Kikan Rironkeizaigaku* XXIII, No. 1, 19-27.

Schumpeter, J.A. and Takata, Y. (1998). *Power or Pure Economics*, Hampshire and London: Macmillan.

Sugihara, T. and Tanaka, T. (ed.) (1998). *Economic Thought and Modernization in Japan*, Cheltenham/Northampton: Edward Edgar.

Sugimoto, E. (1939). *Rironkeizaigaku no Kihonmondai* (The Fundamental Problems of Economic Theory), Tokyo: Nihonhyoronsha.

Sugimoto, E. (1950). *Kindaikeizaigaku no Kaimei* (The Explication of Modern Economics), Tokyo: Iwanamishoten.

Sugiyama, C. and Mizuta, H. (ed.) (1988). *Enlightenment and Beyond, Political Economy Comes to Japan*, University of Tokyo Press.

Takata, Y. (1995), *Power Theory of Economics*, translated by D.A. Anthony, Hampshire: Macmillan.

Tedzuka, J. (1933). *Léon Walras Junsuikeizaigakuyouron* (Léon Walras, Eléments d'économie politique pure), Tokyo: Iwanamishoten.

Yasui, T. (1979). *Keizaigaku to Sonoshuhen* (Economics and its adjacency), Tokyo: Bokutakusha.

Yasui, T. (1980). *Kindaikeizaigaku to Watashi* (Modern Economics and I), Tokyo: Bokutakusha.

Walras, L. (1988). *Elément d'économie politique pure, ou théorie de la richesse sociale, Auguste et Léon Walras, œuvres économiques complètes*, ed. Pierre Dockès et al., Tome VIII, Paris: Economica.

3. Gross Substitutes, Walras' "Rareté" and the Stability of the Middle Class

Hans Maks

Maastricht University, The Netherlands

Abstract

The utility notion of Walras is in essence very similar to the ideas of Jevons and Gossen. The marginal utility (rareté) relations of Walras are decreasing in the quantity and are dependent on only one variable, the "own" commodity.

The reproaches made by latter economists concerning the inadequacy of the formal analysis of Walras to guarantee the uniqueness, the existence and the stability of the equilibrium were never based on this simple utility concept. In this paper we attempt to preliminary analyse the extent of the (in)adequacy again but now closely based upon the essence of Walras' "rareté" relations.

Walras, in contrast with the received opinion, is aware of the uniqueness and stability problem. He maintains that in the groping process stability is a likely property. This paper shows that if, starting from Walras' utility notion, the marginal utility elasticities are larger than minus one, gross stability holds and the stability of the groping process is guaranteed. It is also argued that the elasticity values are more probable smaller than minus one, if the commodity quantities are closer to the existence minimum or closer to the points of satiation.

From this observation it seems likely that in the area between minimum and bliss marginal utility elasticity behaves quiet (>-1) and, hence, stability is obtained. So, evenly distributed endowments or a large group of "middle class" agents increase the likelihood of stable groping processes.

Keywords: General Equilibrium Theory, Utility Notion, "Rareté-relation", Walras

JEL classification: B13, D50

1. INTRODUCTION

Without utility functions or preference relations modern economic analysis would lose its compass and its essence. Especially welfare economics would miss the foundation of its benchmarks. Usually one starts the analysis from an ordinal preference concept in which utility functions can be monotonically transformed.

However, in the early days of the emergence of preference ordering utility was conceived simpler. The utility notion of Walras is in essence very similar to the ideas of Gossen (1854) and Jevons (1879). The marginal utility (rareté) relations of Walras have as most striking simplifying Jevons and Gossen type properties that they are decreasing in the quantity and that they are dependent on only one variable, the "own" commodity.

The reproaches made by latter economists concerning the inadequacy of the formal analysis of Walras to guarantee the uniqueness, the existence and the stability of the equilibrium were never based on this simple utility concept. In this paper we attempt to preliminary analyse the extent of the (in)adequacy again but now closely based upon the essence of Walras' "rareté" relations and specifically to take into account the effects of its simplifying assumptions.

The paper is structured as follows. The next section reviews very shortly Walras utiliy notion emphasising its essential difference with modern utility analysis. Section three deals with the extent of Walras' awareness of the uniqueness and stability properties of equilibria. In section four we relate Walras' "rareté" concept with market gross substitability. The next section (five) concludes that it indeed is likely, as Walras maintains, his groping process is converging to an unique equilibrium. The paper ends with a summarising and concluding section six.

2. WALRAS' UTILITY

Mainstream analysis uses ordinal preferences. Utility functions, describing the ordering of the preferences of an agent can be monotonically transformed. Marginal utility functions are generally assumed to be dependent on all variables. Monotonic transformations can modify decreasing marginal utility in increasing marginal utility and vice versa. Gossen's law of decreasing marginal utility has no meaning at all in this ordinal context. It is replaced by what one might denote as the law of increasing relative satiation. This law implies that indifference "curves" have their regular strictly convex shapes.

In contrast to this ordinal utility notion Walras clearly assumes that his "rareté"-relations, as depicted in his diagrams throughout the Elements, are only dependent on the own commodity and are always decreasing in the quantity of this commodity. This can be seen in all of the graphs in which the "rareté" curves are depicted (see Walras (1954) e.g. p. 118, 119, 123, 176 and 259). One never sees remarks indicating that the position of the "rareté" curves in general shift if the quantities of the other commodities change. Also in the explanation of the attainment of maximum utility, Walras (see (1954) e.g. the explanation of figure 13, p. 123) shows no awareness that the curves in general shift with each exchange or with each change in the initial distribution.

Moreover the "rareté" functions ϕ are always dependent of only one commodity (see (1954) e.g. p. 125). Finally Walras writes total (effective) utility indeed as an addition of effective utilities Φ of each commodity (see (1954) e.g. p. 126). So, it is quite safe to maintain that Walras, in line with founders of the utility concept as Gossen and Jevons and also in line with later authors as Marshall (1890) and Pigou (1923), uses decreasing marginal utility that, moreover, depends only on the own commodity.

We also conclude that Walras bases his formal models on cardinal utility functions that are strongly separable or additive in each commodity.

So, in this paper we use in our analysis of the uniqueness, the existence and the stability of the general equilibrium this simple utility notion. But first we are going to address the question whether Walras was aware of the uniqueness and stability problem in the next section.

3. WALRAS' AWARENESS OF UNIQUENESS

It is the received opinion that Walras is merely counting the number of unknowns and the number of equations and that he is convinced that this solution method is sufficient to guarantee the existence of an unique general equilibrium (strictly positive) price vector (see e.g. Negishi (1989), p. 254.) That counting is not sufficient is well known and since Wald (1936) we have seen quite a number of existence proofs (especially in the fifties) by people like Arrow, Debreu, McKenzie and others.[1] Although these proofs are not too closely related to the models treated by Walras,[2] they share of course a technical and mathematical superiority.

Nevertheless, it should be expressly emphasized that Walras is very much aware that counting is not sufficient as has, very attentively, been observed by van Daal en Jolink (1993). They show a figure (see figure 4.5, p. 26) in which supply and demand in three points intersect. The point in the middle is an unstable equilibrium and does not meet Walras' stability criterion. The other two are locally stable equilibrium points. A similar figure can be found in the Elements (1954) as figure 8a and b, see pp. 110-111.

In discussing the situation depicted in this figure Walras firstly points out that the shape reveals the possibility of several, in this case three, equilibrium points. Then he continues and explains that one of the intersection points is instable because:

> in this case, to the right of this point of equilibrium, the demand for the commodity in question is greater than its offer, which must lead to a rise in price, that is, to a movement farther and farther away from the point of equilibrium. And, in this same case, to the left of the point of equilibrium, the offer of the commodity in

question is greater than the demand for it, which must lead to a fall in price, that is, to a movement once again away of the point of equilibrium.

Walras continues to explain the nature of the other two locally stable equilibrium points. One may be associated with a high quantity and a low price and the other with a small quantity and a high price. From these observations it is safe to conclude that Walras is aware that counting (independent) variables and equation is not sufficient to guarantee the existence of an unique stable equilibrium.

4. WALRAS' "RARETÉ" AND GROSS SUBSTITUTABILITY

The general idea among common economists of what Léon Walras contributed to their science may be summarized with the next system of equations:

$$\mathbf{e}(\mathbf{p}') = 0,$$

in which $\mathbf{e}(\ldots)$ denotes a $(n \times 1)$ vector of excess market demand functions and $\mathbf{p}'$ is a transposed vector of market prices. If the system can be solved for $\mathbf{p}^*$, the system is said to be in a general equilibrium. In all markets, described by the system, if $\mathbf{p} = \mathbf{p}^*$ demand equals supply.

Allais (1943, vol. 2, see pp. 486-489) was the first to demonstrate that gross substitutability between all commodities is sufficient to guarantee uniqueness of the equilibrium and to ensure stability for the groping process (with no off-equilibrium trading). This property implies that the derivatives of the excess demand functions for each good have to be negative with respect to the prices of the other goods.

From the observations in section two we concluded that Walras bases his formal models on cardinal utility functions that are strongly separable or additive in each commodity. In what follows we will clarify what this utility concept implies for the demand equations. Without loss of generality we will start our analysis from the well-known fundamental matrix equation of consumer analysis. From this we have:

$$\partial \mathbf{q}/\partial m = \partial \lambda/\partial m \mathbf{U}^{-1}\mathbf{p}, \tag{1}$$

$$\partial \lambda/\partial m = (\mathbf{p}'\mathbf{U}^{-1}\mathbf{p})^{-1}, \tag{2}$$

$$\partial \mathbf{q}/\partial \mathbf{p}' = \lambda \mathbf{U}^{-1} - \lambda/(\partial \lambda/\partial m)\partial \mathbf{q}/\partial m \partial \mathbf{q}'/\partial m - \mathbf{q}'\partial \mathbf{q}/\partial m, \tag{3}$$

in which $\mathbf{q}$ is the $(n \times 1)$ vector of commodity quantities, λ is the Lagrange-multiplier, $\mathbf{U}$ is the $(n \times n)$ matrix of second order derivatives u_{ij} of the utility function and m is total expenditure.

Since the utility function is additive in the sense that all commodities are independent $u_{ij} = \partial^2 u/\partial q_{ij}^2 = 0, i \neq j, (i, j = 1, \ldots, n)$. Hence, defining $D = \sum p_i^2 u_{ii}^{-1}$ we obtain:

$$\partial\lambda/\partial m = D^{-1}, \tag{4}$$

$$\partial q_i/\partial m = p_i u_{ii}^{-1} D^{-1}, \tag{5}$$

$$\partial q_i/\partial p_j = -\lambda D p_i u_{ii}^{-1} D^{-1} p_j u_{jj}^{-1} D^{-1} - q_j p_i u_{ii}^{-1} D^{-1}, \quad i \neq j, \tag{6}$$

$$D\partial q_i/\partial p_j = -\lambda p_i u_{ii}^{-1} p_j u_{jj}^{-1} - q_j p_i u_{ii}^{-1}, \tag{7}$$

$$D\partial q_i/\partial p_j = (-\lambda p_j u_{jj}^{-1} - q_j) p_i u_{ii}^{-1}. \tag{8}$$

Substitute in (8) $\lambda = u_j/p_j$ to obtain:

$$D\partial q_i/\partial p_j = (-u_j u_{jj}^{-1} - q_j) p_i u_{ii}^{-1}, \tag{9}$$

from which we conclude that gross substitutability holds if

$$-u_j u_{jj}^{-1} - q_j > 0. \tag{10}$$

This can be rewritten as:

$$u_{jj} q_j u_j^{-1} > -1. \tag{11}$$

Hence the marginal utility elasticity $(u_{jj} q_j u_j^{-1})$ should be larger than minus 1 (and of course smaller than zero). This implies that the decrease of the marginal utility should be relative smaller than the relative change in quantity. So an increase in q of say 10% should lead to a decrease of marginal utility of less than 10%.

From these observations we are able to conclude, if we start from Walras' utility concept, that the only thing we have to assume additionally is that the marginal utility elasticities are larger than minus 1. Or that, averaged over the agents, they are such that we have on the market demand level gross substitutability. In the next sections we will analyse how likely it is to have this property on the aggregate level in this simple context. Or to put it in modern terms: what the chances are to have "diagonal dominance" of the own market price effect over the cross price effects.

5. GROPING AND MIDDLE CLASS STABILITY

If the excess demand function values are unequal to zero given a certain value of the prices, Walras proposes the following process of groping of prices to reach general equilibrium. If the excess demand in, say, market 1, is positive we have to rise the price in market 1 such as to obtain a partial equilibrium in that market. This price value is then inserted in the excess demand function of market 2. Next the price in market 2 is adapted such as to equal demand and supply. Next these prices of 1 and 2 are inserted in the excess demand to market 3, market 3 is equilibrated etc. The result is a new price vector.

It is probable, according to Walras (see Elements (1954) p. 172) that this new vector brings the system closer to general equilibrium in the sense that market excess demand functions are closer to zero. Of course, he acknowledges that inserting the partial equilibrium values of the other markets might increase the excess demand values in a part of the markets but in others they may decrease excess demand. So they cancel each other out up to a point. But the decrease must be larger than the increase. Here we already recognize that gross substitutability on the market excess demand level would take care of this.

Going back to the conclusions of the previous section, we know that for a Cobb-Douglas utility function:

$$u = \prod_i q_i^{bi}, \quad \sum_i b_i = 1, \quad i = 1, \ldots, n, \tag{12}$$

with cardinal utility and $u_i > 0$ and $u_{ii} < 0$ for $\forall i$, we have $0 < b_i < 1$. Hence this preference function satisfies the condition (11), because the marginal utility elasticities equal $-b_i$ for $\forall i$. So if we would insert for Walras' utility the Cobb-Douglas specification, everything would be OK, assuming positive endowments. But even in the simple Walras' utility context Cobb-Douglas seems a bit too restrictive choice.

Another simple utility function satisfying Walras' utility notion is

$$u = \prod_i (q_i - \mathrm{c}_i)^{bi}, \quad \sum_i b_i = 1, \quad i = 1, \ldots, n. \tag{13}$$

It generates the well known LES. Here we see that things are a bit more complicated. If $0 \geqslant \mathrm{c}_i$, $\forall i$, we have gross substitutability. But positive values of c_i are to be interpreted as committed quantities. This means that they can be seen as existence minimum quantities, say, to survive. Only above these value the choice problem is relevant for the agent. If $\mathrm{c}_i > 0$, gross substitutability holds if $q_i > \mathrm{c}_i b_i^{-1}$. If we are in the neighbourhood of the committed quantity (more precisely $c_i < q_i \leqq c_i b_i^{-1}$) gross substitutability is not obtained. This means that the marginal utility elasticity has a strong negative value (<-1). In terms of economic intuition one might explain this as follows. The first units of a commodity above its minimum quantity contributes significant to the agents utility, but this significant initial increase decreases fast, leading to the relative strong negative value of the marginal utility elasticity.

In general one might say that this characteristic has some appeal: an increase of quantities close to the minimum may generate a lot of utility but this increase decreases fast. On the other hand: the further away we are from the minimum, the more likely it is that the marginal utility elasticity has the proper value to generate gross substitutability.

From this insight the following generalizing step might not be too daring: the more agents in an economy equipped with Walras' rareté's are close to the committed quantities for more commodities, the more markets will not reveal gross substitutability and the more unstable markets one may expect. But the further away the agents are from these quantities the more likely it is, up to a point as we shall see in a moment, that gross substitutability is obtained.

Now, if we take the (diagonal) quadratic utility function:

$$u = \sum_i q_i c_i + 0.5 a_{ii} q_i^2, \quad c_i > 0, \quad a_{ii} < 0, \quad i = 1, \ldots, n,$$

and define $b_i = -a_{ii}^{-1} c_i$, we note that the $(n \times 1)$ vector $\mathbf{b}$ with elements b_i indicates the point of satiation. Gross substitutability holds if $q_i < 0.5 b_i$. Hence, we observe that the closer we are in the neighbourhood of this bliss point $\mathbf{b}$ the more likely it is that the gross substitutability commodity property is lost. This indicates again that the marginal utility elasticity has a strong negative value (<-1).

In terms of economic intuition one might explain this as follows. If we approach the point of satiation for a commodity the decrease in utility increases. Bliss comes in an increasing speed. This leads to the relative strong negative value of the marginal utility elasticity.

In general one might again say that this characteristic has some appeal: if the quantity of a commodity neighbours or approaches satiation, an increase of quantities may lead to a relative fast decrease of marginal utility. From this observation the following generalizing step appeals: the more agents in an economy equipped with Walras' rareté's are close to the point of satiation for more commodities, the more markets will not reveal gross substitutability and the more unstable markets one may expect. But further away from bliss, we likely obtain more gross substitutability.

Hence, combining the two arguments above, we conclude that the closer we are to minimum or to bliss, the more likely we do not have gross substitutability. But in the area between minimum and bliss marginal utility elasticity likely behaves quiet (>-1) and generates stability.

If we relate this observation to the endowment distribution over the agents in this economy we note that the more evenly it is, the more it is between bliss and minimum, the more stability we likely have in the economy. To put it in a slightly different perspective the Walras economy is likely to be more stable the larger the class of middle class agents is and the smaller the groups of poor and very rich agents. The stability of a Walras economy is served by a relative large "middle class".

Walras maintains as we have seen that it is likely that the "groping" of the price vector brings the system closer to general equilibrium in the sense that market excess demand functions are closer to zero. Now we observe that this is likely to happen the more "in the middle" Walras' economy is in terms of the extent that agents are away from minima and bliss points.

6. CONCLUSION

We have seen that Walras, in contrast with the received opinion, is aware of the uniqueness and stability problem. He maintains that in the groping process stability is a likely property. This paper shows that if, starting from Walras' utility notion, the marginal utility elasticities are larger than minus one, gross stability holds and the stability of the groping process is guaranteed. It is also argued that the elasticity values are more probable smaller then minus one if the commodity quantities are closer to the existence minimum or closer to the points of satiation.

From this observation it seems likely that that in the area between minimum and bliss marginal utility elasticity behaves quiet (>-1) and, hence, stability is obtained. So, evenly distributed endowments or a large group of "middle class" agents increase the likelihood of stable groping processes.

This result generates support for ordo-liberal insights. Especially W. Röpke (1946, see esp. p. 239 a.f.) and W. Eucken (1949) emphasise that within the economic order not only sufficient competition (vollständige Konkurrenz) should be strived at but also a just income distribution.

NOTES

1. For reviews of existence proofs see Arrow and Hahn (1971) and Weintraub (1985).
2. See e.g. Van Daal en Jolink (1993), p. 160.

REFERENCES

Allais, M. (1943). *Traité d'économie politique pure*, 2 vols. Paris, Imprimerie Nationale.

Arrow, K. and Hahn, F.H. (1971). *General Competitive Equilibrium*. Amsterdam, North-Holland.

Debreu, G. (1959). *Theory of Value, an Axiomatic Analysis of Economic Equilibrium*. New Haven, Yale University Press.

Daal, J. van and Jolink, A. (1993). *The Equilibrium Economics of Léon Walras*. London, Routledge.

Eucken, W. (1949), Die Wettbewerbsordnung und ihre Verwirklichung, *ORDO*, Bd. 2, p. 1 a.f.

Gossen, H.H. (1854). *Entwicklung der Gesetze der menschlichen Verkehrs und der daraus fliessenden Regeln für menschliches Handlen*. Braunschweig, Vieweg.

Jevons, W.S. (1879). *The Theory of Political Economy*. London, Macmillan (2nd ed.).

Marshall, A. (1890). *Principles of Economics* (ed. by C.W. Gillebaud), 2 vols. London, Macmillan.

Negishi, T. (1989). *History of Economic Theory*. Amsterdam, North-Holland.

Pigou, A.C. (1923). *Essays in Applied Economics*. London, Macmillan.

Röpke, W. (1946). *Die Lehre von der Wirtschaft*. 4. Auflage, Erlenbach-Zürich, Eugen Rentsch.

Wald, A. (1936). "Über einige Gleichungssysteme der Mathematischen Ökonomie". *Zeitschrift für Nationalökonomie*, 7, 633-670.

Walras, L. (1954). *Elements of Pure Economics or the Theory of Social Wealth* (translated from the 1926 definitive edition by W. Jaffé). London, G. Allen & Unwin.

Weintraub, E.R. (1985). *General Equilibrium Analysis; Studies in Appraisal*. London, Cambridge University Press.

4. Léon Walras and the English Classical School: Walras's Production Theory Revisited

Yukihiro Ikeda

Keio University, Japan

Abstract Conventional wisdom holds that the ideas of Walras and the other two stars of the Marginal Revolution, William Stanley Jevons and Carl Menger, are diametrically opposed to the English Classical School. However, the view that their formal models are in all respects anti-Classical in nature is debatable. I contend that Walras's production theory in particular is closely related to the English Classical School.

Keywords: Léon Walras, Adam Smith, Production Theory, Marginal Revolution, English Classical School, *Tâtonnement* Process

JEL classification: B31

1. INTRODUCTION

Léon Walras's *Eléments d'économie politique pure* is widely regarded as a cornerstone of modern economics, having served as a source of insight for such eminent scholars as J.R. Hicks, P.A. Samuelson, Kenneth Arrow, and Gerard Debreu, to name only few. As a Japanese historian of economic thought, I would furthermore argue for the importance of *Eléments* as an influence on at least two prominent Japanese economists, namely Hirofumi Uzawa and Michio Morishima.

Conventional wisdom holds that the ideas of Walras and the other two stars of the Marginal Revolution, William Stanley Jevons and Carl Menger, are diametrically opposed to the English Classical School. However, the view that their formal models are in all respects anti-Classical in nature is debatable. I contend that Walras's production theory in particular is closely related to the English Classical School, for the following four reasons:

1. In Walras's model, entrepreneurs do not make profits or suffer losses. Thus, prices in the long run tend to approach natural prices, in keeping with the models of the Classical School.

2. In Walras's so-called *tâtonnement* process, the free entry or exit of firms is assumed. This assumption brings to mind the conception of firms described in such works of the English Classical School as *The Wealth of Nations*.
3. In the typical Arrow-Debreu model, firms are allowed to use their capital and labour as they like, whereas in *Eléments* the ratio between various factors is simply given. Thus, Walras's production theory shares one of the basic characteristics of the English Classical School: it is a fixed-coefficient model.
4. Walras was ambivalent with regard to the marginal productivity theorem, for reasons closely related to the preceding point. Although he attempted to capture the essence of the theorem, he did not rewrite his production theory in accordance with this recent development in economic theory. As he put it:

> I preferred ... not to introduce the theory of marginal productivity into my general theory of economic equilibrium, for fear that the general theory, which was already complicated enough, might then be too difficult to grasp in its entirety. (Walras, 1977: 385)

Indeed, as shall be shown, Walras's formal model is not compatible with the marginal productivity theorem.

For these reasons, I argue in this paper for locating Walras's *Eléments* within the tradition of the English Classical School. As a foundation for this argument, I present in the following section a rather formal picture of what Adam Smith described verbally in the *Wealth of Nations*. In the third section, I attempt to clarify the basic theoretical structure of Walras's production theory vis-à-vis Smith and the formal models of the English Classical School. To avoid possible misunderstandings concerning the relationship of Walras and Smith, three closely interrelated yet distinct perspectives must be differentiated here: (1) Smith's and Walras's own interpretations of their respective models; (2) The formal relationship between the Smithian and Walrasian models, viewed objectively with modern tools including mathematical reformulations; and (3) Walras's views on Smith. With regard to this third perspective, W. Jaffé notes that "Walras's *Eléments* mentions the *Wealth of Nations* only twice: to criticize Smith's alleged definition of economic science and to denounce as a sophism Smith's labour theory of value" (Jaffé, W. [1977/1993]: 159). Jaffé is quite correct in maintaining that "Walras's blindness to all he had in common with Adam Smith is traceable, in part at least, to his oft-expressed anglophobia" (Ibid.: 159). To prevent Walras's severe criticism of Smith from obscuring the common ground shared by these two masters of political economy, this section exclusively concerns the first two of these three perspectives. In the fourth section, I present a brief survey of the views of Walras's contemporaries on his production theory, before concluding with remarks that summarize and qualify my findings in this paper.

2. *WEALTH OF NATIONS*: MARKET PRICE AND NATURAL PRICE

Let us consider a formalized view of several well-known ideas from the *Wealth of Nations*. First, Adam Smith defines "natural price" as follows:

> When the price of any commodity is neither more nor less than what is sufficient to pay the rent of the land, the wages of the labour, and the profits of the stock employed in raising, preparing, and bringing it to market, according to their natural rates, the commodity is then sold for what may be called its natural price. (Smith, 1976: 72)

As shall be shown, natural price as Smith defines it corresponds to what Walras refers to as the "cost of productive services." Smith defines market price as follows:

> The market price of every particular commodity is regulated by the proportion between the quantity which is actually brought to market, and the demand of those who are willing to pay the natural price of the commodity, or the whole value of the rent, labour, and profit, which must be paid in order to bring it thither. (Ibid.: 73)

Typical of eighteenth and nineteenth century thinkers before J.S. Mill, Smith does not clearly consider equilibrium conditions, but rather focuses on the proportions of supply and demand. Nonetheless, let us suppose that market price is given by the following simple equation:

$$D(p) = S, \tag{1}$$

where p is market price, D is a demand function of consumers, and S is a given quantity of a commodity. Short-run equilibrium can be obtained by solving Equation (1) for p. Long-run equilibrium can be defined as follows:

$$D(n) = S, \tag{2}$$

where n represents natural price. Equation (2) can be interpreted as determining S, the long-run supply level of the commodity.

Next, let us consider Smith's description of the process of adjustment that ensues when natural price is higher or lower than market price as defined above:

> If at any time it exceeds the effectual demand, some of the component parts of its price must be paid below their natural rate. If it is rent, the interest of the landlords will immediately prompt them to withdraw a part of their land; and if it is wages

> or profit, the interest of the labourers in the one case, and of their employers in the other, will prompt them to withdraw a part of their labour or stock from this employment. (Ibid.: 74-75)

As Smith outlines it here, this dynamic process can be described by the following equation:

$$S(t+1) = S(t) + u(p(t) - n), \quad u > 0, \tag{3}$$

where $S(t)$ is the supply level in a given period, $S(t+1)$ is the supply level in the next period, and n is the natural price in the sense defined above. If the market price of a commodity is higher or lower than the natural price, output will increase or decrease, respectively, in the next period. u denotes the speed of adjustment.

The demand function of consumers can be specified simply, as follows:

$$D(p) = a + bp, \quad b < 0. \tag{4}$$

By combining these two equations, we obtain the following:

$$S(t+1) = S(t) + u((S(t) - a)/b - n). \tag{5}$$

A simple calculation reveals that as t tends towards infinity, $S(t)$ converges with $a + nb$ under the following condition:

$$-1 < u/b < 0.$$

Considering the signs of u and b, this condition can be rewritten as:

$$|b| > |u|.$$

It follows that if the speed of adjustment does not outstrip the slope of the demand function, then the system will remain stable. Under this condition, supply level will converge with demand level in correspondence with natural price, and market price will converge with natural price, as Smith maintained.[1]

3. WALRAS'S PRODUCTION THEORY: ZERO PROFITS FOR ENTREPRENEURS

In Walras's model, entrepreneurs neither make profits nor suffer losses. When a condition of profit or loss arises, the responses of other entrepreneurs restore it to zero.

For the case of profit conditions, Walras outlines two possible responses by which equilibrium is restored. First, if entrepreneurs are making profits in a given field, other entrepreneurs will rush into this field to share their profits. Alternatively, existing firms will simply increase their production. Walras summarizes these two possibilities as follows:

> If the selling price of a product exceeds the cost of the productive services for certain firms and a profit results, entrepreneurs will flow towards this branch of production or expand their output, so that the quantity of the product will increase, its price will fall, and the difference between price and cost will be reduced... (Walras, 1977: 225)

Once again, Walras explains that either existing firms will increase output to meet demand in a given field, or that other firms will move into the field, changing the overall number of firms in this field in the process.

Walras offers a corresponding argument for the case of loss conditions:

> If the cost of the productive services exceeds the selling price for certain firms, so that a loss results, entrepreneurs will leave this branch of production or curtail their output... (Ibid.: 225)

Parallel to the two possibilities for conditions of profit, two different responses are also possible in the case of loss conditions: either existing firms will simply reduce output, leaving the overall number of firms in a field unchanged; or entrepreneurs will leave the field for other businesses.

In contrast to these contentions from Chapter 18 of *Eléments*, Walras's arguments in Chapter 21 mention only increases and decreases in output by existing firms in a field, making no reference to the possible entry or exit of firms in response to profit or loss conditions:

> Given several services by means of which various products can be manufactured and assuming that these services are exchanged for their products through the medium of a *numéraire*, for the market to be in equilibrium, or for the prices of all the services and all the products in terms of the *numéraire* to be stationary, it is necessary and sufficient (1) that the effective demand for each service and each product be equal to its effective supply at these prices; and (2) the selling prices of the product be equal to the cost of the services employed in making them.... [If the second condition (2) is not satisfied], [i]t is necessary to increase the output of those products the selling price of which is greater than the cost of production and to decrease the output of those products of which the cost of production is greater than the selling price. (Ibid.: 253-254)

Once again, only the possibility of increases and decreases in output by existing firms in a given field is at stake in Walras's argument here. He does not explicitly mention the possibility that the overall number of firms in the field may change.

Walras describes this dynamic adjustment process in similar terms in his preface to the fourth edition of *Eléments*, in which he considers his theory in relation to the work of other contemporary economists:

> These entrepreneurs will expand output whenever the selling price of the products exceeds the cost of the productive services involved in their production; and they will reduce their output whenever the cost of these productive services exceeds the selling price. (Ibid.: 41-42)

As in his argument in Chapter 21, Walras again omits mention of the movement of firms from one sector to the other.

Yet there are passages in *Eléments* other than those in Chapter 18 in which Walras does explicitly describe the movement of firms. In Chapter 22, for example, Walras describes the conditions under which the principle of free competition prevails.[2] The second of these conditions concerns the importance of the equalization of selling price and the cost of production. He explains this condition as follows:

> A second foundation on which our proof rests is the equalization of the selling prices of products with their costs of production. Our proof, consequently, presupposes that it is possible for entrepreneurs to enter profitable businesses and to withdraw from those operating at a loss. (Ibid.: 257)

As this quotation demonstrates, Walras does explicitly return to the possibility of the entry and withdrawal of firms to and from a given field in response to conditions of profit or loss.

It is commonly understood that the assumption of free entry and free exit is essential to the concept of perfect competition. Models of the English Classical School rely on this assumption, but how about the Walrasian model?

Let us first consider the Arrow-Debreu model, which represents a modern version of Walras. In contrast to models of the English Classical School, the Arrow-Debreu model does not explicitly account for the possibility of free entry and free exit. Producers are expected to maximize profits within the constraints of technology, but not beyond these constraints. As Hiroaki Osana rightly observes, "the entry or exit of a producer belongs to problems in the long-run" (Osana, 1987: 1). In contrast, "the Arrow-Debreu formulation of competitive equilibrium may be looked upon as concerning short-run equilibrium" (Ibid.: 1).

The condition of the equalization of profit – that is, of zero profit across business sectors – is a characteristic of the English Classical School, which is based on a concern with assumption of long-run equilibrium. Obviously, the condition of zero profit across sectors is not satisfied in the Arrow-Debreu model. Some firms make profits and others neither make profits nor suffer losses. Those firms that do make profits distribute them to consumers according to a predetermined ratio. Since the possibility of non-activity is included in the production possibility set, firms that suffer losses are excluded from Arrow-Debreu. In any case, the condition of zero profit is not satisfied in this modern Walrasian model.

Does this conclusion apply, however, to the original model represented in *Eléments*? As shown above, Walras does explicitly allow for the free entry and exit of firms, at least in Chapters 18 and 22, though elsewhere he does not refer to this possibility. If Walras – even ambiguously – admits the possibility of free entry and exit, this implies a close relationship between his model and those of the English Classical School.

Furthermore, in both Walras's *Eléments* and the models of the English Classical School, the condition of zero profit is satisfied, a natural consequence of the allowance of free entry and exit. As Donald Walker puts it, Walras "dealt with the long run ... [and] ... did not, in the formal structure of his mature model, concern himself with the conditions of short-run equilibrium in production" (Walker, 1996: 289). Walker's evaluation is fully compatible with my analysis here.

Let us now consider a formalized version of Walras's production theory. The following equations describe the essence of this theory for a one-commodity, one-factor case:

$$ax = r(w), \tag{6}$$

$$aw = 1, \tag{7}$$

$$x = r(w)w. \tag{8}$$

x represents demand for the commodity, and serves as *numéraire*; as such the price of x is equal to one. a is the quantity of the factor that is used to produce one unit of the commodity. w is a factor price such as wage rate. $r(w)$ is a supply function of the factor. Equation (6) is a demand-supply condition of the factor. Equation (7) indicates that the price equals the cost required to produce one unit of the commodity. Equation (8) is the budget constraint of the consumer.

Since these three equations are not independent, Equation (8) can be dropped, reducing the system to the following two equations:

$$ax = r(w), \tag{9}$$

$$aw = 1. \tag{10}$$

These two conditions are sufficient to determine a, final demand, and w, wage rate. In this simple system, w is determined only by the technical condition, independently of the demand condition.

Turning now to the dynamics of the system, the adjustment process can be described by the following two equations:

$$w(t+1) = w(t) + u(ax(t) - r(w(t))), \tag{11}$$

$$x(t+1) = x(t) + u(1 - aw(t)), \tag{12}$$

where $w(t)$ is the wage rate of this period, and $w(t+1)$ denotes that of the next period. If there is an excess of demand or supply, the wage level will increase or decrease, respectively, in the next period. Furthermore, if the price level is higher or lower than the natural level, output will increase or decrease, respectively, in the next period. u denotes the common adjustment speed.

A supply function of labour can be specified as follows:

$$r(w(t)) = \alpha + \beta w(t), \quad \beta > 0. \tag{13}$$

The linear supply function of Equation (13) can be obtained by maximizing the following problem. Let us assume an additive utility function of the form:

$$U(r, x) = F(l - r) + x, \quad \text{where } F(l - r) = b(l - r) - c(l - r)^{1/2}, \tag{14}$$

l denotes a given parameter, for instance, 24 hours. Thus, $l - r$ is the time remaining for leisure in a given 24-hour period. Maximizing this function subject to the budget constraint of Equation (8) yields the following labour supply function:

$$r = b/(2c) + l + w/(2c). \tag{15}$$

It is evident that Equation (15) is a linear function of wage level. In the following, let us assume Equation (13), the microfoundation of which is Equation (14). That is, if a utility function is additive and the marginal utility of the commodity is constant, then the supply function of labour can be expressed in the form Equation (13).

Based on this assumption, long-run equilibrium can be defined as follows:

$$ax^* = \alpha + \beta w^*, \tag{16}$$

$$1 = aw^*. \tag{17}$$

Eigenvalues of the above system can be obtained as follows:

$$\mu = ((2 - u\beta) + u(\beta^2 - 4a^2)^{1/2})/2,$$

$$\nu = ((2 - u\beta) - u(\beta^2 - 4a^2)^{1/2})/2.$$

If $\beta^2 > 4a^2$, both roots are real. Furthermore, if $-1 < \mu < 1$ and $-1 < \nu < 1$, the system is stable. That is, $w(t)$ and $x(t)$ converge to w^* and x^* as t tends to infinity. If $\beta^2 < 4a^2$, the roots are complex. Furthermore, if $(1 - u\beta + u^2a^2)^{1/2} < 1$, the movements will be damped with oscillations.

Consider the following numerical example: $\alpha = 0$, $\beta = 2$, $a = 0.5$, $u = 1$. In this case, $w^* = 2$, $x^* = 8$. If $w(0) = 1$ and $x(0) = 1$, then the wage and output in the following period can be easily calculated. This example satisfies $\beta^2 > 4a^2$, $-1 < \mu < 1$, and $-1 < \nu < 1$.

Now consider another numerical example: $\alpha = 0$, $\beta = 1$, $a = 0.8$, $u = 1$. In this case, $w^* = 1.25$, $x^* = 1.5625$ and the movements are damped with oscillations.

Finally, let us consider the more general multi-commodity, multi-factor case, which can be described as follows:[3]

$$Ax = r, \tag{18}$$

$$A'w = p, \tag{19}$$

$$x = f(p, w), \tag{20}$$

$$r = r(p, w). \tag{21}$$

A denotes a matrix of coefficients of production. A' denotes a transposed matrix of A. Equations (18) and (19) correspond to Equations (6) and (7), respectively. x is a vector showing demand functions of each commodity. r is a vector showing supply functions of each factor. These equations can be solved for x, r, p, and w. It is generally agreed that the existence of the above equations is warranted under certain conditions.[4]

4. WALRAS'S PRODUCTION THEORY AS HIS CONTEMPORARIES SAW IT[5]

As shown above, an essential characteristic of Walrasian production theory is that it is a system based upon fixed coefficients of production. This can be interpreted as an assumption of constant returns to scale, as many economists of Walras's era recognized. The following consideration of their views on Walras relies on the *Revue d'économie politique* of 1890, in which numerous arguments concerning *Eléments* appeared.

Predictably, the publication of the second edition of *Eléments* in 1889 gave both friends and enemies of Walras an opportunity to scrutinize his doctrines anew. First, a friendly review in *Revue* by Ladislas Bortkevitch – whom Walras, in his correspondence with Luigi Perozzo, described as a young man with talent – defended Walras from the harsh criticism of Edgeworth, an eminent

British mathematical economist at the time. In his short review, Bortkevitch characterizes Walrasian economics as follows:

> Je crois, pour ma part, qu'une bonne théorie de l'économie politique doit compter avec le fait de l'égalité des prix de vente aux prix de revient, car, autrement, elle serait incomplète; et je crois, en outre, que le système de M. Walras satisfait parfaitement à la condition requise. (Bortkevitch, 1890: 83)

Bortkevitch captures the essence of Walrasian economics admirably, pointing out that its production theory relies on the condition that prices tend to approach costs in the long run. This condition is a typical characteristic of the models of the English Classical School.

From a similar perspective, Austrian economists Rudolf Auspitz and Richard Lieben (well-known as the authors of *Untersuchungen über die Theorie des Preises*) respond to Walras's production theory critically, stating the following in an article in *Revue*:

> Nous au contraire, nous étudions soigneusement l'accroissement du coût de production et par là du prix de revient avec l'augmentation de la quantité fabriqueé; nout trouvons que cet accroissement est plus que proportionnel, et qu'en tenant compte de nos suppositions, le prix de revient monte de quantité à quantité. (Auspitz and Lieben, 1890: 603)

Auspitz and Lieben assert that the cost of production increases with the output of a commodity, and that the marginal cost increases with the output. These characterizations differ markedly from those offered above of the Walrasian model. Simply put, Auspitz and Lieben's argument here is based on the marginal cost principle, whereas what Walras has in mind is the average cost principle. Auspitz and Lieben continue:

> Même alors le prix ne descend qu'au prix de revient de l'entreprise la plus faible, tandis qu'il rest toujours un gain de production aux entrepreneurs situés dans de meilleures conditions. Nous ne pouvons donc admettre ni l'égalité du prix de vente, qui est unique pour tous, avec le prix de revient, qui diffère d'une entreprise à l'autre, ni la négation du gain de production, qui est le mobile le plus actif de toute entreprise. (Ibid.: 603)

The model that Auspitz and Lieben describe can be explained by the following simple equation determining output level:

$$MC(x) = p \tag{22}$$

MC denotes a marginal cost curve. Output level, x, is determined at the point where the marginal cost equals the given price, p.

Such a description comprises nothing more than the explanations of an introductory microeconomics textbook. As the Auspitz and Lieben quote reflects, output level is equivalent to the number of firms in a given field. There is room for firms for which $MC < p$ to make profits. Only in the case of firms for which $MC = p$ does the Walrasian condition hold that entrepreneurs neither make profits nor suffer losses.

Dutch economist Anthony Beaujon, an insightful critic of Walrasian economics, addressed the same point in his review of *Eléments* in *Revue*:[6]

> Voilà le trait d'union entre le prix du marché et le rix de revient; trait d'union don't M. Walras donne dans son livre un exposé mathématique ce fait: *qu'il n'y a pas de prix de revient general; qu'il n'y a que des prix de revient individuels, de même qu'il n'y a que des valeurs d'usage individuelles.* (Beaujon, 1890: 22)

For Beaujon, costs differ from firm to firm, depending on the productivity of each producer. This assumption is incompatible with the Walrasian conception of cost described above. Walras simply does not deal with differences in cost structure between firms. Beaujon offers the example of agriculture, a sector in which the importance of differences in productivity is obvious enough:

> Enfin, en ce qui concerne spécialement l'entreprise agricole, les differences de productivité naturelle et de situation du sol constituent une cause puissante de differences de prix de revient du produit agricole. (Ibid.: 23)

In their respective emphases, these neat characterizations of Walras by economists of his era lend support to my analysis in the foregoing sections. That is, what we observe in the discourse of Walras's nineteenth century contemporaries is a conflict between the average cost principle – represented by both the English Classical School and Walras – and the marginal cost principle. Although Auspitz and Lieben as well as Walras are considered forerunners of modern economics, they pursued different paradigms with regard to production theory.

5. CONCLUDING REMARKS

Although Walras was a pioneer of modern microeconomics, his production theory is related to the English Classical School insofar as the models of both are based on fixed coefficients of production as well as the average cost principle. At the same time, Ricardian economics can also be seen as an application of the marginal principle, as has been widely noted; I do not deny the role of the marginal principle in Classical economics, a subject too complicated to be interpreted from the perspective of one simple principle. Thus, my assertion in this paper is rather modest: in regard to the average cost principle, both Walras and the English Classical School share a common understanding of how price and output are determined. This assertion implies a greater robustness than that commonly attributed to the English Classical School of the second half of the 19th century.

NOTES

References to the *Wealth of Nations* are from *the Glasgow Edition of the Works and Correspondence of Adam Smith*. English translations of excerpts from Walras's *Eléments* are drawn from Walras (1977).

1. For a graphical exposition see Mizuta (1989).
2. For restrictions on the laissez-faire principle in *Eléments* and other works, see Jolink (1996:107-114). The following arguments draw on Jolink's explanations. For a broader, more detailed account of Walras's conception of the entrepreneur, see also Misaki (1998: 37-58).
3. The following formulation is from Fukuoka and Koyama (1959).
4. For a detailed discussion OR analysis of the existence problem of Walrasian production theory, see, for example, Fukuoka and Koyama (1959); and Van Daal, Henderiks and Vorst (1985/1993).
5. This section draws heavily on Walker (1996: 288-301) as well as on Jaffé's footnotes in Walras (1965: 1889, n. 1, 3), which provided the biographical information on Beaujon, among other insights.
6. According to Jaffé in Walras (1965: 1889, n. 3), this article is a reproduction of Anthony Beanjou, "Wiskunde in de economie", In *De Economist*, 1889, Vol. 38, 613-629.

REFERENCES

Auspitz, R. and Lieben, R. (1890). "Correspondance." *Revue d'economie politique* 4, November-December, 599-605.

Beaujon, M.A. (1890). "A propos de la théorie du prix." *Revue d'economie politique* 4, January-February, 16-42.

Bortkevitch, L. (1890). "Bulletin bibliographique." *Revue d'economie politique* 4, 80-86.

Debreu, G. (1959). *Theory of Value*. New York: Wiley.

Fukuoka, M. and Koyama A. (1959). "Reexamination of the General Equilibrium Theory à la Cassel." (In Japanese) *Kikan Riron Keizaigaku*, 9(1/2).

Jaffé, W. (1977/1993). "A Centenarian on a Becentenarian: Léon Walras's *Eléments* on Adam Smith's *Wealth of Nations*." *Canadian Journal of Economics* 10(1), 19-33. (Reprinted in John Cunningham Wood (ed.), *Leon Walras, Critical Assessments*, Vol. 1, *The Life of Léon Walras and Perspective on his Thought*. London and New York: Routledge, 159-174.)

Jolink, A. (1991). Liberté, Egalité, Rareté, the Evolutionary Economics of Léon Walras: an Analytical Reconstruction. Amsterdam: Tinbergen Instituut.

Jolink, A. (1996). *The Evolutionist Economics of Leon Walras*. London and New York: Routledge.

Misaki, K. (1998). *Economic Thought of Walras: Social Vision of General Equilibrium Theory* (In Japanese). Tokyo: Nagoya University Press.

Mizuta, K. (1989). "Classical Economics: Market, Classes, and Capital Accumulation." (In Japanese) In Ikuo Ohmori (ed.), *Economic Thought of Market and Money*. Tokyo: Shouwado.

Morishima, M. (1977). *Walras's Economics: a Pure Theory of Capital and Money*. Cambridge: Cambridge University Press.

Osana, H. (1987). "Long-run Equilibria For Perfectly Competitive Markets." *Keio Economic Studies*, 24(1), 1-11.

Smith, A. (1976). *The Glasgow Edition of the Works and Correspondence of Adam Smith, I, Vol. 1, An Inquiry into the Nature and Causes of the Wealth of Nations*. Oxford: Oxford University Press.

Van Daal, J., Henderiks, R.E.D. and Vorst, A.C.F. (1985/1993). "On Walras's Model of General Economic Equilibrium." In *Zeitschrift für Nationalökonomie* 45(3), 219-244. (Reprinted in John Cunningham Wood (ed.), *Léon Walras, Critical Assessments*, Vol. 2, *Walrasian Economics*. London and New York: Routledge, 366-388.)

Van Daal, J. and Jolink, A. (1993). *The Equilibrium Economics of Léon Walras*. London and New York: Routledge.

Walker, D. (1996). *Walras's Market Models*. Cambridge: Cambridge University Press.

Walras, L. (1965). *Correspondence of Léon Walras and Related Papers*, William Jaffé (ed.), Vol. 2, 1884-1897. Amsterdam: North-Holland Publishing Company.

Walras, L. (1977). *Elements of Pure Economics or the Theory of Social Wealth*, translated by William Jaffé. Fairfield: Ausgustus M. Kelley Publishers.

5. Léon Walras's Economics*: From Pure to Normative?

Jan van Daal

Le Fau Haut, 15600 Boisset, France

Abstract The Leitmotiv of Léon Walras's work was his desire to contribute to the solution of what he called the Social Question. The fact that so many people were living in misery was unacceptable to him. So, it is not amazing that his *Études d'économie sociale* and *Études d'économie politique appliqué* are thoroughly normative; even the *Éléments* may be considered as normative, at least as written with normative intentions. In this paper this is exemplified by a discussion of Walras's monetary work, preceded by an explanation of his views on science in general and economics as part of social science in particular and further discussed in the last section.

Keywords: Léon Walras, Normative Science, General Economic Equilibrium, Monetary Economics

JEL classification: B13, B31

1. INTRODUCTION

As we all know, the Leitmotiv of Léon Walras's (1834-1910) work was his desire to contribute to the solution of what he called the Social Question. The fact that so many people were living in misery was unacceptable to him.

His study for becoming a mining engineer must therefore be considered as a false start. Given his aim, and his Bohemian temper, his failure at the École des Mines was inevitable. His first steps as a man of letters formed the second false start. His novel *Francis Sauveur* (1858) and his short story "La Lettre", together with some unpublished or untraceable essays can only be considered as tragic. The novel (a sugary, burdensome love-story) is preceded by an in-

---

*Since this paper contains many citations from Léon Walras's *Études d'économie politique appliquée*, it might make sense to point to the fact that after the presentation of this paper in 2002 an English translation of the just mentioned book appeared: Léon Walras, *Studies of Applied Economics*, translated and introduced by Jan van Daal, London: Routledge, 2005.

troduction of 35 pages, in fatiguing italics, devoted to the social question and related topics. Apparently, the author vainly tried to serve two lords at the same time: Literature and the Social Question.

Auguste Walras (1801-1866) put his son on the right track by persuading him that the best thing to do was devoting his life to social science, in particular to economics, since for solving the social question it was first necessary to identify exactly the problem's context and nature, which might be found in economics. Convinced, guided and inspired by his father, Léon Walras plunged into social science. By nature, he was a man who wanted to do the things starting from the very beginning. Therefore, he set out to formulate his own answers to a number of questions. What is science? What is social science? What is, in particular, economic science as related to social science? The answers have provided him with a systematic research programme for the rest of his life: a sort of filing system in which each thing he devised could find a logical place. Moreover, Walras's set-up provided a time schedule and prescribed an order of research projects to be undertaken.

Below I shall first briefly discuss Walras's view on science in general and economics in particular, leading to his schemes for doing research. Further, I shall make plausible by means of the example of his treatment of money, that Walras's blood, too, was thicker than water. He did applied work upon a weak, premature theoretical basis and his final theoretical work contradicted more or less that applied work. This could mean that the schemes presented below might rather be a result of ours, men of hindsight, in our attempt to make things more beautiful than they really were.[1] Further, we shall see that what Walras called his applied economics, is highly normative; as it should be, he says.

2. SOCIETIES AND ITS SCIENCES

For Walras, the starting point of economic research was the fact that people are living in a given society and that they depend on each other because everyone has his own specialization. I may elucidate this by the following scheme, the idea of which dates from 1867. It expresses that, according to Walras, there are two main categories in society to be distinguished, studied, analyzed and co-ordinated: things and persons (*Théorie générale de la société*, 2nd lesson; 1990: 49 ff.; see also Jolink, 1996: 68).

Pure economics, Walras said, deals with nature, causes and laws of social wealth; applied economics deals with this wealth's production. Social economics, also called moral economics by Walras, deals with the repartition of social wealth among the members of society. It has to do with both social wealth and human rights.

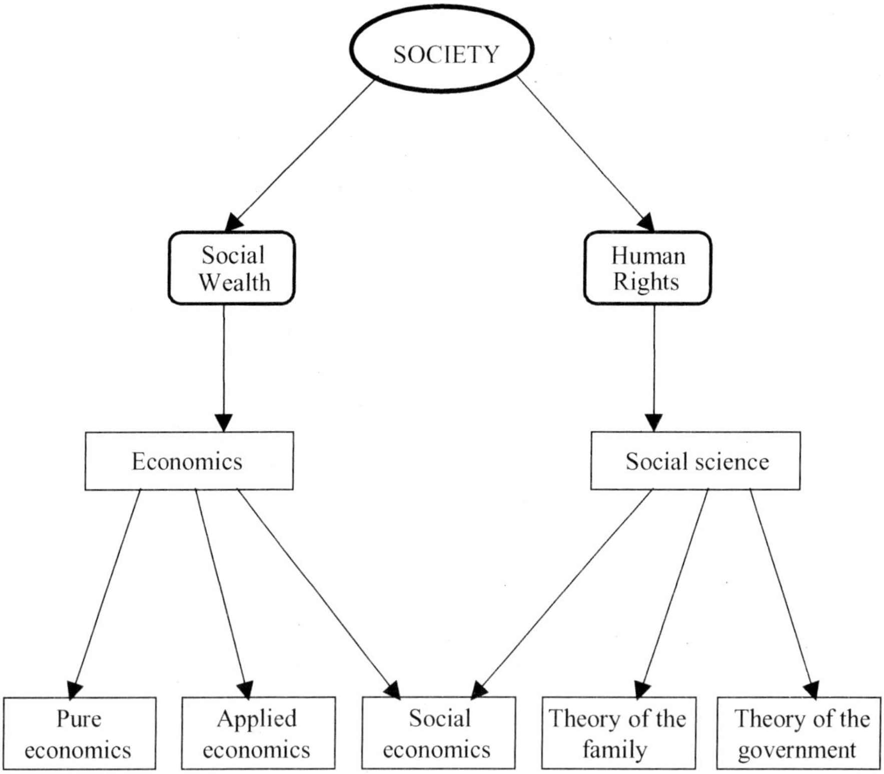

Figure 1. Society and its sciences.

The scheme above interferes with two other schemes, Tables 1 and 2 below. Table 1 explains Walras's ideas on the classification of science in general and Table 2 specifies this for economic science.

The idea behind this scheme is explained by Walras at several places throughout his work. In his *Mélanges d'économie politique et sociale*, for

Table 1. Walras's classification of science

		Sciences	
		Pure	*Applied*
Object	*Nature*	*Pure natural sciences*	——
	Persons, vis-à-vis nature	*Pure moral sciences*	*Applied natural sciences*
	Persons, vis-à-vis persons		*Applied moral sciences*

instance, the following passage, dating from 1879, can be read (1987: 414; Walras's italics):

> *Pure* science establishes facts and relations; *applied* science prescribes rules of conduct. There exist *pure natural* sciences, studying facts and relations which have their origin in the play of the fatal forces of nature and *pure moral* sciences, studying facts and relations originating from the exercise of the free will of man [...]. There exist *applied natural* sciences, providing rules of conduct for man vis-à-vis impersonal things and *applied moral* sciences, providing rules of conduct for people vis-à-vis each other.

The upper right cell of the scheme is necessarily empty because it does not make sense to speak about rules of conduct for nature vis-à-vis itself.[2]

Pure sciences are for instance mathematics, physics, chemistry and philosophy. Examples of applied natural sciences (dealing with the relation Man-Things) are geodesy, pharmacology and medicine. Applied moral sciences (dealing with the relations Man-Man) are, for example, law, ethics and theology. Applied sciences must be preceded by and based upon one or more pure sciences.

From Part I of the *Éléments*, it seems that Table 1 has overruled Figure 1. So, according to Walras it was not simply pure theory vs. practice. There are rather three stages:

Pure theory — Applied theory, or theory of the art.[3] — Practice of the art.

3. ECONOMICS

In economics, Walras says, the main phenomenon to explain is exchange of things, material or immaterial, both useful and limited in quantity. Walras reserved the adjective "scarce" for these things, whose entirety he called "Social Wealth".[4] The phenomenon of exchange is closely linked to three others: (1) value in exchange (price), (2) production, or industry, which can be seen both from both a technical and an economical point of view, and (3) property.

In Walras's opinion, value in exchange is a natural fact because it originates from the natural limitations of quantities of things, independent of our psychological freedom. This does not mean that we do not have any control over prices as natural facts. Just as we respect the laws of gravity, we should respect the laws of exchange, since we are unable to change them. In Walras's scheme, both property and industry arise from the exercise of human will. Industry belongs to the category of manifestations of human will on natural forces. Property is a manifestation of human will on other people's will or actions. See also *Éléments*, §19 (1988: 41-2). For economic science, Table 1 can then be specified into the following scheme:

Table 2. Walras's classification of economics

<table>
<tr><th></th><th></th><th colspan="2">Economics</th></tr>
<tr><th></th><th></th><th>Pure</th><th>Applied</th></tr>
<tr><td rowspan="3">Object</td><td>Nature</td><td>Pure natural economics</td><td>——</td></tr>
<tr><td>Persons, vis-à-vis nature</td><td rowspan="2">Pure moral economics</td><td>Applied natural economics</td></tr>
<tr><td>Persons, vis-à-vis persons</td><td>Applied moral economics</td></tr>
</table>

The bulk of Walras's scientific work can be found in his three main treatises: *Éléments d'économie politique pure, ou Théorie de la richesse sociale* (1874, 1669, 1896, 1900), *Études d'économie sociale (Théorie de la répartition de la richesse sociale)* (1896) and *Études d'économie politique appliquée (Théorie de la production de la richesse sociale)* (1898), further to be called for short *Éléments*, *EES* and *EPA*. They can be placed in a table deduced from the one above:

Table 3. Walras's three treatises within the framework of Table 2

<table>
<tr><th></th><th></th><th colspan="2">Texts</th></tr>
<tr><th></th><th></th><th>Pure economics</th><th>Applied economics</th></tr>
<tr><td rowspan="3">Object</td><td>Nature</td><td>Éléments d'économie politique pure, ou Théorie de la richesse sociale</td><td>——</td></tr>
<tr><td>Persons, vis-à-vis nature</td><td rowspan="2">Etudes d'économie sociale (Théorie de la répartition de la richesse sociale), Part I</td><td>Etudes d'économie politique appliquée (Théorie de la production de la richesse sociale)</td></tr>
<tr><td>Persons, vis-à-vis persons</td><td>Etudes d'économie sociale, Parts II, III, IV</td></tr>
</table>

These schemes do not only indicate the relationships between the various components of Léon Walras's research, but they seem to impose also a certain order with respect to their timing. If in certain applied work one needs some theory, then that theory must exist already. We shall see that in the case of Walras's work on applied monetary theory, indeed, he made use of theory he developed before. However, he also used elements (like the "economic tides") that lacked theory and he did not always revise applied work in the light of further development of his own theory.

4. PURE NINETEENTH-CENTURY THEORY AND MONEY

April 3, 1903 Walras wrote to Louise Georges Renard (Walras, 1965, L. 1543):

> If one wants to obtain quick results one should grow carrots and salad, but if one has the ambition to plant oaks one should be so wise as to say by oneself: "Later generations will be grateful to me for this shelter."

I think that Walras, indeed, planted an oak. Jolink and I decorated the cover of our *Walras's Equilibrium Economics* (1993) with a picture of that oak. Figure 2 is an "update" of it. The tree has grown from the seed of utility, sown in the beginning of the seventies of the nineteenth century. Exchange of two goods is its trunk. There is a branch of barter, not further developed. From the branch of exchange with money as a means of payment, two branches of production come out: first, the nineteenth-century branch of production, with tâtonnement allowing for production in disequilibrium, secondly, the twentieth-century branch in which Walras changed his "real tâtonnement" into his tâtonnement sur bons. The latter can be found in all the twentieth-century models (exposed in the fourth edition of the *Éléments* (1900). The nineteenth-century models with capital formation have all so-called empirical savings functions. This means that these functions have been posited by Walras as unspecified functions of prices and the rate of interest and put directly into the models instead of deduced from optimizing behaviour of the economic agents. When extending these models with money, Walras followed the same procedure in presenting "empirically" the aggregate of the consumers' desired cash-balances, expressed in prices and the rate of interest. These monetary general equilibrium models leaned heavily on a crude form of the quantity theory.[5] The quantity theory lies also at the basis of what we called Walras's monetary macro model, to be set out below.

Before dealing with the rest of the tree, I continue with some short remarks on the nineteenth-century monetary models. First a citation concerning Walras's intentions with regard to the nature of fiat-money money on the one hand and commodity-based money on the other (*Éléments*, editions 2 and 3, §320; 1988: 452):

> For pure theory it is obviously advantageous to investigate [first] how something gets value when it becomes money, before exploring how this value as money has to be combined with value as merchandise.

This quotation makes clear that Walras considered fiat-money models rather as a pedagogical expedient.

Consumers and producers need money for transactions and saving. The total amount of this money is called "cash balance", indicated by the symbol H. It

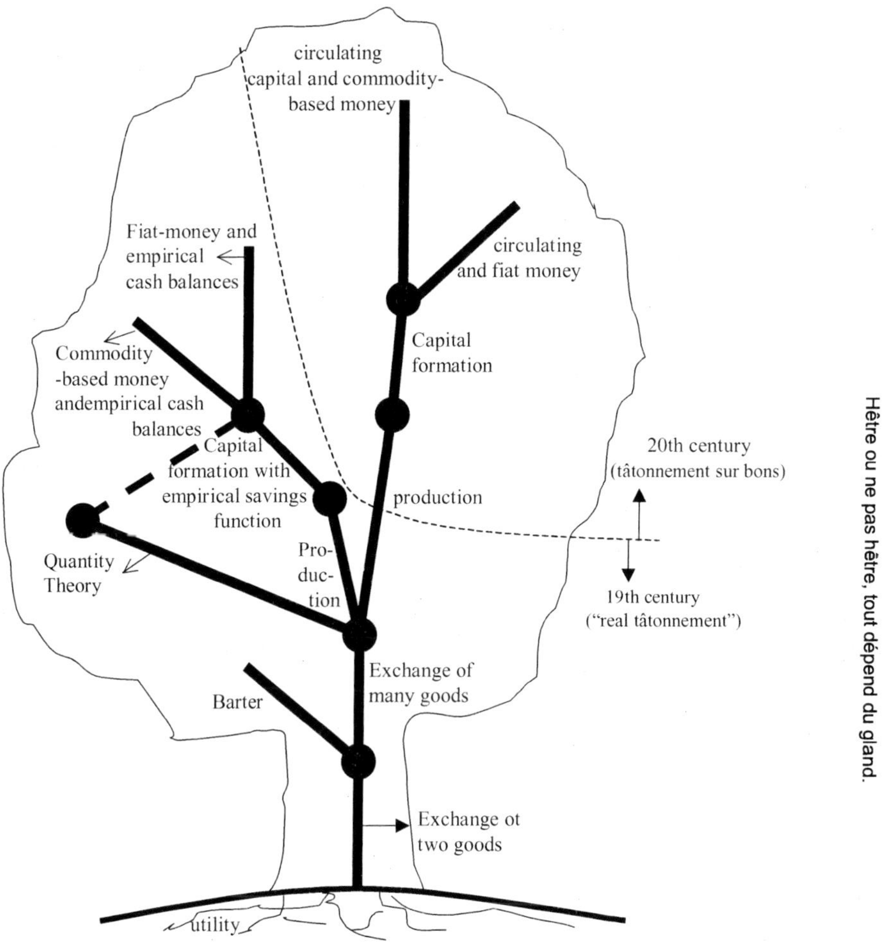

Figure 2. Walras's oak.

depends on existing practical circumstances and needs felt by the economic agents. In editions two and three of the *Éléments* this total cash balance is simply expressed in some non-monetary numéraire (B) as a linear function of the prices of all goods and services. Subsequently, this is plugged in into the monetary models of general economic equilibrium. Let the good (U) be money. Given its quantity Q_u, the price p_u of money, expressed in numéraire, follows from the quantity theory: $Q_u p_u = H$. The goods and services' money prices follow then from dividing all the prices in terms of the numéraire by p_u.

Walras's macro money-model for the explanation of the price of money when some precious metal serves both as money and commodity, will be set out by means of a graphical analysis that can be found at several places in his works. See Figure 3, borrowed from *EPA* (1992: 342).

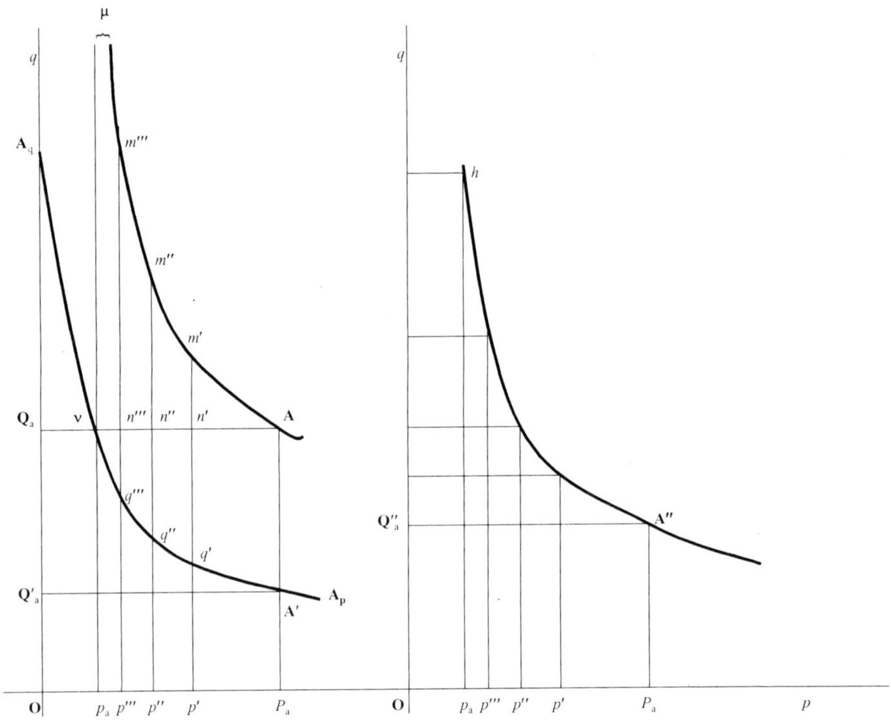

Figure 3. The price of money.

Let (A) be the money commodity and let its total quantity in the economy be Q_{a}, separated in a quantity Q'_{a} as merchandise and a quantity $Q''_{\mathrm{a}} = Q_{\mathrm{a}} - Q'_{\mathrm{a}}$ as money. Let P_{a} be the price of (A) as money and commodity. In line with what has been said about the total cash-balance, Walras simply put: $Q''_{\mathrm{a}} P_{\mathrm{a}} = H$, where H was predetermined, i.e. independent of P_{a}. Furthermore, the analysis seems to suggest that he considered only two goods (A) and (B), or considered (B) as representing in some way all goods other than (A); see lesson 26 of the first edition and lesson 15 of the other editions of the *Éléments* (1988: 233-42).

The curve passing through A′ in Figure 3 is the graph of the demand function $q = F_{\mathrm{a}}(p)$. Hence, it displays for each price p of (A) in (B) the total quantity of (A) as a commodity demanded if p is the prevailing price. In the right-hand side of the figure the orthogonal hyperbola with equation $q = H/p$ is represented. The curve through A in the left-hand side is the result of the vertical addition of the two just mentioned curves. Now it can easily be read from the picture how p shifts from p_{a} to P_{a} if (A) becomes money.

5. NINETEENTH-CENTURY APPLIED MONETARY THEORY

In the ideal situation envisaged by Léon Walras, where misery belongs to the past, prices should not fluctuate unexpectedly, haphazardly. Therefore, he proposed a system of *global* price control. No particular price should be controlled or prescribed, but measures should be taken such that the price system as a whole will "behave well". For that reason Walras used the macro monetary model exposed above to underpin his well-known project for monetary reform. In addressing himself to the meeting of the Latin Union (a monetary union formed by Belgium, France, Greece, Italy and Switzerland), he said it as follows (1992: 16-17, italics added):

> The monetary unit is the franc, that is to say $^{10}/_{31}$ of one gramme of gold of an alloy of $^{9}/_{10}$ fine.
>
> The MONEY will consist of gold 10 and 20 francs coins. These will be minted by the State on the request of private persons. Minting may be neither suspended nor limited.
>
> Independently of the gold money, there will be double silver token:
>
> 1° A FRACTIONAL token consisting of silver coins of $2^{1}/_{2}$, 5 and 10 grammes of silver of an alloy of $^{835}/_{1000}$ of a nominal value of $^{1}/_{2}$, 1 and 2 francs;
> 2° A REGULATING token consisting of écus, namely silver coins of 25 grammes in an alloy of $^{9}/_{10}$ fine, of a nominal value of 5 francs.
>
> The silver token should be minted by the State; it will only circulate within its issuing country and only be accepted for payments up to a certain amount. The quantity of token that may be issued by each of the States forming the Latin Union will be determined by international conventions. This should be done, as far as the fractional token is concerned, for the sake of circulation, for small payments, and, as regards to the regulating token, *for assuring a regular variation in the value of money*. Every State of the Union will profit from the benefits and bear the losses coupled with the issue or withdrawal of its token.

In many papers, Walras went at length to explain this "open-market policy avant la lettre". He thereby introduced the ephemeral notion of the "economic tides", borrowed from Jevons. This can be inferred from the following long citation, taken from Walras's *Théorie de la monnaie* (1992: 68-69):

> It is quite certain that the curves of variation in prices of a certain number of commodities, subjected to normal variations in utility and quantity must form a confusing tangle. But in order to find out whether or not one may emphasise the phenomenon of the economic tide, one has to derive from these specific curves the general, or average curve by taking precautions, if need be, with respect to the commodities affected by exceptional circumstances. [...] Jevons did [this] in two cases: in the memoir entitled "A Serious Fall in the Value of Gold Ascertained and its Social Effects Set Forth" (1863)[6] for the period 1845-1862, and again in another memoir entitled "The Variation of Prices and the Value of the Currency since 1782" (1865)[7] for the period 1782-1862. In both cases, the phenomenon

> of the economic tide is clearly apparent. I do not know of any French statistician who has made a study of this subject which may be opposed to Jevons's investigations, but on the contrary, I have very recently had the pleasure of noticing that the conclusions of the English economist are confirmed by French observations. According to Jevons, the undulations of the curve of the average price of commodities corresponding to the movements of the economic tide agree with those of the exchange rate at the Bank of England. Mr. Jacques Siegfried presented, in *Le Temps* of 1st February last, a graph of the two curves of securities [commercial securities, treasury bills not included] and the amount of cash in the Banque de France [gold and silver], during the period 1847-1885, according to which the economic tide distinguishes itself as clearly as possible, high tide and ebb appearing when the curve of the security is at its maximum and beginning to descend whereas the curve of the amount of cash is at its minimum and beginning to rise; low tide and flood appear when the curve of the securities is at its minimum and beginning to rise whereas the curve of the amount of cash is at its maximum and beginning to descend. Since the economic tide really does exist both in France and England, how can one possibly doubt that it has an effect on prices?

The monetary authorities should be well aware of the moments of ebb and flood of the economic tides. Therefore, Léon Walras pleaded for better statistics in this respect. He gave thereby many practical hints. Further, he stressed some fundamental ideas. Highly important, he said, is the fact that the issue of banknotes can lead to instability. In his "Théorie mathématique du billet de banque" (dating from 1879), he went at length in analyzing the nature of banknotes and in exposing some of their disadvantages. He ended this article as follows (1992: 341):

> The issue of banknotes has more inconveniences than advantages. This will even be the case if we suppose, as we did, that all phenomena accompanying or succeeding it take place in a normal way. However, what should one say now if one believes that it would never come true that way! We supposed the banknotes issued exclusively by institutions of short-term credit as a representation of good commercial papers. At present, however, we may them as well consider as issued by institutions of long-term credit as representation of mortgage loans or unsecured loans. We may suppose them issued by institutions of short-term credit representing revolving credit or accommodation bills. Anyway, they are no longer absolutely reimbursable, neither at presentation, nor within a delay of ninety days. We have supposed the issue to take place slowly and progressively. Consequently, the depreciation of money, the demand for new capital goods, the rise of the prices will be slow and progressive as well. However, if one now supposes that all these phenomena manifest themselves abruptly and excessively, would then the issue of banknotes unquestionably be nothing else than making ready an indeterminate crisis of exchange? If one attentively thinks over these contingencies, one would shiver more and more with respect to that dangerous instrument of credit called banknote.

This citation is representative for Walras's opinion about banknotes and their use.

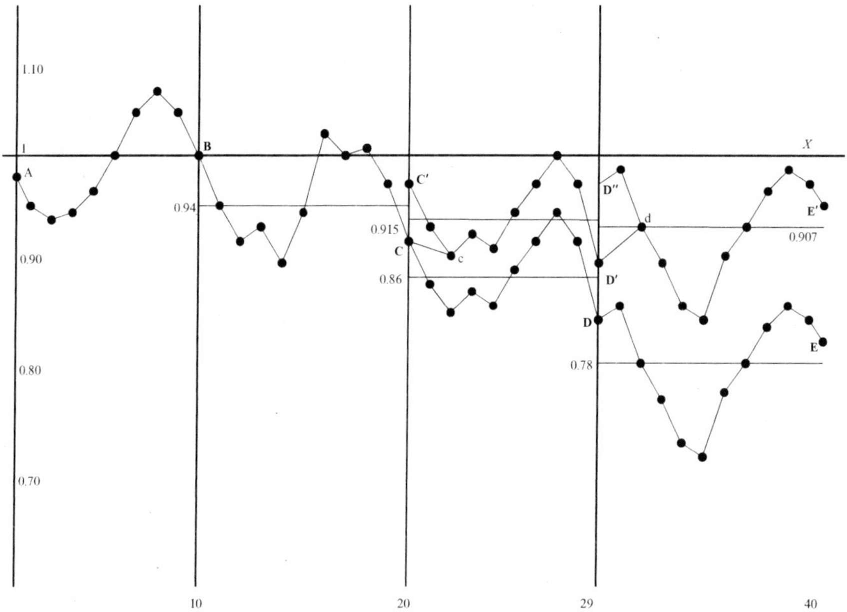

Figure 4. Introduction of regulating token at time 20 and at time 29.

The economic tide is according to Walras a natural phenomenon that should not be influenced as such. It is the variation of the tide that should be managed. See Figure 4 (1992: 144). Without the introduction of regulating token the price-level would have been represented by the curve ABCDE. Introduction of it at the right moments would result into the curve ABCcD′dE′.

Another issue of importance in this respect is formed by Walras's ideas on mono-metallism and bi-metallism. As often, here also he takes a middle position, which made him unpopular in all champs. The following citation, dating from 1886, makes this clear (1992: 138):

> The final result of this whole study is that the greatest possible stability of the prices cannot be obtained by trying to find it in a single one of the four systems, gold-monometallism, silver-monometallism, bimetallism, regulating token, but by making an alternating use of all four.... One should imagine the four systems as placed in the following order [...]:
>
> Silver-monometallism — Bimetallism — Regulating token — Gold-monometallism.

6. TWENTIETH-CENTURY PURE MONETARY THEORY

The twentieth-century part of the oak of figure 2 will now be discussed. From the fourth edition of his *Eléments* onwards (lesson 23, §242), Léon Wal-

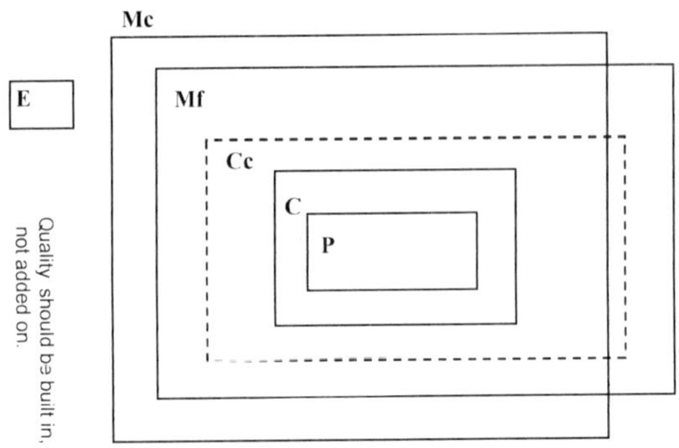

Figure 5. Walras's equilibrium models.

ras introduced a theory of savings into the model of capital formation based on individual utility maximization. The model of capital formation was thereafter expanded into two models, one with circulating capital and fiat money and one with circulating capital and commodity-based money. The notions of circulating capital and money as a special kind of circulating capital were elaborated in the fourth edition of the *Eléments* (lesson 29; 1988: 443 ff.); the demand for and supply of circulating capital and money were thereby formally derived as resulting from individual decision making. Walras's treatment of his fourth-edition models of circulating capital and money is highly complicated; it is condensed in the twelve pages of lesson 29 of the last two editions of the *Eléments*. Therefore, we have introduced elsewhere[8] a walrasian "model of circulating capital"; an extension of the model of capital formation, to be inserted between the latter model and the money models of Walras's chain. Just as all models, except the one with commodity money, of Walras's chain, the model of circulating capital is to be considered as a pedagogical tool; from this one can easily derive Walras's money models.

Considering a model as a collection of symbols forming a number of equations, the mutual connection between Léon Walras's models of general economic equilibrium can be illustrated by the Venn diagram of Figure 5, where **E** denotes the model of exchange, **P** the model of production, **C** the model of capital formation, **Cc** the model of circulating capital, **Mf** the model with fiat-money, and **Mc** the model with commodity-based money. The model of exchange lies isolated from the other models in the diagram because mathematically the model of production is not a generalization of it. Walras himself was of the opinion that each of the models **E**, **P**, **C** and **Mf** was completely embedded in the following one of his chain **E**-**P**-**C**-**Mf**-**Mc**. This is not the case; see Van Daal 1994 and 1998.

One of the additional features of the new set-up of the models with money is that in the models of the last two editions of the *Éléments* money is no longer "added on", but has really been built in into the model. Another new aspect, in connection with the just mentioned one, is that Walras introduced the fact that paying is something that costs money, because one makes use of a special type of circulating capital.

The use of money for paying and for other purposes is based upon the preferences of the consumers and the technical circumstances in the enterprises. This means that not any trace of the quantity theory is left in the model. The quantity of commodity money has become endogenous and there is no reason for prices to vary in proportion to it. This means that Walras's applied monetary theory is not supported by the last developments of his pure theory. See Van Daal and Jolink (1993b, pp. 105-106) and Van Daal (1994).

7. DISCUSSION: NORMATIVE ECONOMICS

The classical economists regarded, roughly spoken, the workers together with the wretched persons (the paupers) as one grey mass. In equilibrium, each member of this class just receives the minimum wage, according to the standards of time and place. However, if one wants to elevate these people to conditions that are more favourable,[9] one must devise a theoretical economic framework in which each person, or at last each family, is considered as a separate entity, because everyone's happiness counts. Walras did so in his pure theory by presenting the hypothesis of the utility maximizing consumer and his theory of general economic equilibrium under the regime of free competition, the former being the cement in the latter. This part of his research is well known, and his fame rests on it.

Most economists, indeed, have restricted their attention to the *Éléments* only, in particular to its last edition (the posthumous one, 1926). There are several reasons for this nearly exclusive attention. First, Walras himself attached much care to the *Éléments*, as appears from the fact that during his lifetime he published four editions of the book, altering, rearranging and supplementing it every time. He himself presented it as his most important work. Obviously, the subject of general economic equilibrium was never out of his mind.

Secondly, the 1926 edition of the *Éléments* is the only one of Walras's books that has been translated into English until now (by William Jaffé, 1954). Thirdly, as so many first-generation academic economists, Walras felt (and indeed was) obliged to provide an overall picture of the whole field. Starting with pure theory, however, he ran out of time and did not succeed in completing the two other treatises he envisaged.[10] Instead, he consolidated the bulk of his other research in the *EES* and the *EPA*. In the form of a collection of already existing papers they could not compete with the *Éléments* and therefore the latter book received most of the attention.

The *five* editions of the *Éléments* and the two *Études* contain the essence of Walras's work. There are four main conclusions to be drawn from these books:

1. In his *analytical economics* of free competition Walras was thinking in terms of what we call now temporary equilibrium. This means that he stylised economic life into consecutive periods during which trade and production, as well as saving and capital formation take place as described by a carefully devised mathematical model explaining general economic equilibrium per period, given some initial situation. Capital, including money was to carry over value from period to period and economic growth was to be brought about by saving.
2. Though Walras was thinking in terms of subsequent periods, he devoted most of his attention to what happens during a period, leaving the transition from period to period at the background of his thinking. In the first three editions of the *Éléments* his mathematical models were really dynamic in that, among other things, they tried to describe how production and trade, starting from some initial situation of endowments, were groping during the period in question to a state of equilibrium.

   In the fourth edition, he abandoned every trace of this dynamic approach and supposed production and trade only to take place, instantaneously, in a state of equilibrium (see Walker, 1996 and Van Daal, 2000).
3. In his theory of *applied economics* and in his *social economics* Walras considered the elements needed for the completion of the mathematical theory of economic equilibrium. He considered thereby the possibility of equilibrium beyond the strict boundaries imposed by free competition and the traditional institutions. He did so because contributing to a solution of the Social Question was his aim. His economics, therefore, was primarily intended to provide instruments within the framework of this broader design, namely to unfold an optimal economic order and produce prescriptions for reaching this ideal.
4. An explicit exposition of this broader design never saw the light. Nevertheless, it is possible to make a plausible conjecture how such a scheme could have looked like if Walras would have been given the time and the mental energy to work it out himself. In fact, such a scheme should be considered as the blueprint of Walras's normative economics.

There has been some discussion about the nature of Walras's books. Whatever the answer may be, the *EES* and the *EEA* are thoroughly normative. In these two books Léon Walras dealt extensively with monopoly and other market organizations, with public goods, taxation and ownership, in particular State ownership of the land; it was always his intention to insert these elements in what he called his *complete mathematical theory of economic equilibrium* (*EES*, p. 433; 1990: 400). As already has been indicated above, he paid so much attention to pure theory that he ran out of time and the synthesis was never achieved.

Some time ago an attempt has been made to fill this lack.[11] It was found that the above-mentioned broader design maybe synthesized in "*general* general economic equilibrium models" in which the above elements have been inserted. They can be fashioned such that they have the same mathematical structure as the models discussed in the *Éléments*. This is not too surprising because, firstly, the assumption of constant returns to the scale of production, expressed in the assumption of fixed coefficients of production, is maintained and hence marginal costs and average costs will always coincide. Secondly, the abolition of taxation combined with State ownership of the land and the fiction of a social-welfare function has the effect that the State has a real budget constraint with rent as its income. The State plays, therefore, a role that mathematically does not differ from that of an individual. Consequently, regarding optimality, these extended models do not differ from the models exposed in the *Eléments*. I believe that these models form a blueprint of the ideal situation envisaged by Walras. The *Éléments*, indeed, are mainly positive.

I think to have made clear all this by means of the schemes and the examples presented above. Of course, Walras did not start as a positive economist to evolve gradually into normativism. This follows easily from his earlier publications (Walker, 1987). As so many pioneering scientists, he zigzagged through the field. As a conclusion, we may say that, ultimately, Walras's economics appears altogether normative. He was thereby a man with, what I should like to call a "static vision" on the progress of society, a Cartesian "après la lettre".

NOTES

1. All the material about the classification of (economic) science below has been developed in first instance within the framework of the research for Jolink's doctoral dissertation (Rotterdam, 1991, in particular Chapter 3). Many topics of the rest of this paper where devised when we were working on our joint undertakings, under wonderful circumstances, indeed; see Jolink (1996, page x).
2. Jolink (1991, Figure 3.1, p. 60) gave the table a slightly different form:

<table>
<tr><td></td><td></td><td></td><td colspan="2">Method</td></tr>
<tr><td></td><td></td><td></td><td>Pure</td><td>Applied</td></tr>
<tr><td rowspan="3">Fact</td><td colspan="2">Nature</td><td>Pure nat. sc.</td><td></td></tr>
<tr><td rowspan="2">Persons</td><td>vs. nat.</td><td rowspan="2">Pure moral sc.</td><td>Applied nat. sc.</td></tr>
<tr><td>vs. persons</td><td>Applied moral sc.</td></tr>
</table>

3. The latter word is meant in the same meaning as in the word "artisan".
4. *Éléments*, Preface (1988: 11). In first instance, Walras was not as explicit about the distinction between flows and stocks as was already Adam Smith. The latter's *Wealth of Nations* begins with words that are highly interesting, in particular to the econometrician: "The *annual* labour of every nation..." (Smith, 1994, p. lix; our emphasis). Walras must certainly have read this.
5. Walras's attempts to prove the (his) quantity theory rigorously cannot be considered as completely successful. See, for example, the appendix to his *Théorie de la monnaie* (1992: 146-151).
6. "A serious fall in the value of gold ascertained and its social effects set forth" (1863), chapter ii of *Investigations in Currency and Finance*, London: Macmillan, 1884, pp. 34 *ff.*
7. William Stanley Jevons, "The variation of prices and the value of the currency since 1782" (1865) in *op. cit.*, pp. 119-150.
8. Van Daal and Jolink (1993b, chapter 13); see also Van Daal (1994).
9. I do not say that the classics did not aim so.
10. *Éléments d'économie sociale* and *Éléments d'économie politique appliquée*, books meant to be just as elaborate and methodical as the *Éléments d'économie politique pure*, but they never saw the light.
11. Van Daal and Jolink (1993a and 1993b, pp. 120-126); see also Van Daal (1999).

REFERENCES

Jolink, A. (1991). *Liberte, égalité, rareté,* Doctoral dissertation, Erasmus Universiteit Rotterdam.

Jolink, A. (1996). *The Evolutionist Economics of Léon Walras*, London: Routledge.

Smith, A. (1994) [1776]. *An Inquiry into the Nature and Causes of the Wealth of Nations*, New York: The Modern Library.

Van Daal, J. (1994). "De la nature de la monnaie dans les modèles monétaires de l'équilibre général économique de Léon Walras", *Économies et Sociétés*, Série Oeconomia, Histoire de la Pensée Économique, PÉ, n° 20-21: 115-132.

Van Daal, J. (1998). "Léon Walras's general economic equilibrium models of capital formation: existence of a solution", *Revue Économique* 49, 1998, pp. 1175-1198.

Van Daal, J. (1999). "Léon Walras et le capitalisme", *Revue européenne des sciences sociales*, Tome XXXVII, n° 116, pp. 83-99.

Van Daal, J. (1999). "Les tâtonnements dans le modèle de la production chez Léon Walras. Bons à rien?", in L'économie walrasienne, Actes du Colloque de l'Association Internationale Walras, 16 septembre 1999, *Les Cahiers du CERAS* (Reims), Hors-série n° 1, juin 2000, pp. 58-78.

Van Daal, J. and Jolink, A. (1993a). "On Walras's 'general general equilibrium model' ", in R.F. Hebert (ed.), *Perspectives on the History of Economic Thought*, Vol. IX, Aldershot: Edward Elgar Publishing Company, Ch. 9.

Van Daal, J. and Jolink, A. (1993b). *The Equilibrium Economics of Léon Walras*, London and New York: Routledge.

Walker, D.A. (1987). "Bibliography of the Writings of Léon Walras", *History of Political Economics* 19 (4): 667-702.

Walker, D.A. (1996). *Walras's Market Models*, Cambridge: Cambridge University Press.

Walras, L. (1858). *Francis Sauveur*, Paris: E. Dentu.

Walras, L. (1859). "La Lettre", *Revue Française*, Vol. 16, pp. 193-206, 275-285.

Walras, L. (1954). *Elements of Pure Economics, or the Theory of Social Wealth*, translated and annotated by W. Jaffé. Homewood, Ill: Irwin; London: Allen and Unwin.

Walras, L. (1965). *Correspondence of Léon Walras and Related Papers*, 3 vols, edited by William Jaffé. Amsterdam: North-Holland Publishing Company.

Walras, L. (1987). *Mélanges d'économie politique et sociale*, edited by Claude Hébert et Jean-Pierre Potier, under the auspices of the Centre Auguste et Léon Walras at Lyon, Vol. VII of *Auguste et Léon Walras: Œuvres économiques complètes*, Paris: Économica. (Not published during his lifetime.)

Walras, L. (1988). *Éléments d'économie politique pure, ou théorie de la richesse sociale*, variorum edition of the editions of 1874, 1877, 1889, 1896, 1900 and 1926 (and of the edition of the Abrégé de 1938) augmented by a translation of the notes of William Jaffé in Elements of pure economics (1954), edited by Claude Mouchot, under the auspices of the Centre Auguste et Léon Walras at Lyon, Vol. VIII of *Auguste et Léon Walras: Œuvres économiques complètes*, Paris: Économica.

Walras, L. (1990). *Études d'économie sociale (Théorie de la répartition de la richesse sociale)*, edited by Pierre Dockès, under the auspices of the Centre Auguste et Léon Walras at Lyon, Vol. IX of *Auguste et Léon Walras: Œuvres économiques complètes*, Paris: Économica. (First edition 1896, second edition 1938.)

Walras, L. (1992). *Études d'économie politique appliquée (Théorie de la production de la richesse sociale)*, edited by Jean-Pierre Potier, under the auspices of the Centre Auguste et Léon Walras at Lyon, Vol. X of *Auguste et Léon Walras: Œuvres économiques complètes*, Paris: Économica. (First edition 1898, second edition 1938.)

6. What Went Wrong with Walras? The Econometric Transformation Process of Walrasian Economics during the 1920s and 1930s

Albert Jolink

Erasmus University Rotterdam, The Netherlands

Abstract

This paper will address the issue of the reception and transformation of Léon Walras's work among some econometricians during the 1920s and 1930s. As set out in the paper, the reception of Walras's work is related to the importance of the role of statistics, the dynamic representations of a changing reality and the consistency of simultaneous equations modelling.

The main contribution of this article lies perhaps in detecting these (different) reasons 'what went wrong with Walras' but should also be seen in the light of an extrapolated discussion of the current relevance of Léon Walras work and his legacy for modern political economy.

The conclusion is that the reception of Walras's work by the early econometricians (statisticians and mathematicians together) was lukewarm, partly because it represented the wrong ideas and partly because of ignorance. When and where Walras's work was discussed it was mainly as a starting point to illustrate the relevance of the changes suggested by the newly founded econometric discipline. At the end of the day, this may illustrate the development of the economic discipline, but perhaps even more importantly it may reveal the need for weaving Walras's applied and social economics into our present-day Walrasian texture.

Keywords: Walras, Statistics, Econometrics, Economic Dynamics

JEL classification: B13, B23, B31

1. INTRODUCTION

In the Spring of 1908 Henry Ludwell Moore asked Léon Walras's opinion "as to the wisdom of attempting, by modern statistical methods, to bring a number of conclusions of pure economics to a statistical test."[1] Walras's attitude towards statistics is now well documented (Ménard, 1980) and may explain why Moore's question remained unanswered: the limited amount of statistical work Walras was involved in and the limited fields of application, illustrate the subordinate role of statistics in his work. Hence, with the rise of the use statistics in economics in the early 20th century, the work of Walras offered little to hold on to.

With the emergence of econometrics in the 1920s and 1930s, however, some need for justification of their work was felt by the early econometricians and was found by stressing the antecedents. But as Mary Morgan has indicated, "although the econometricians of the 1930s were to refer to their tradition as that of Cournot, Walras and Marshall, any simple derivation of econometrics from the neoclassical programme is highly dubious, not least because it ignores the important inputs from empirical economics."[2]

Walrasian theory was largely ignored during the first decades of the 20th century.[3] In France, Walrasian theory experienced a simmering existence, kept alive due to massive efforts of Walras's daughter, Aline. In the U.K. most of the developments in mathematical economics were achieved independently of Walras's work; in Switzerland and Italy most of the Walrasians were converted into Paretians. Possibly the strongest trait d'union in the first decade of the 20th century was found at Columbia University, through Henry L. Moore.

But even Moore recognized that Walras's representation of interrelatedness of economic relations through a static system of simultaneous equations was the means rather than the ends to further economics and that transformations were required. According to H.L. Moore's utopia (*Synthetic Economics*), 'synthetic economics' would consist of "(1) the use of simultaneous equations to express the *consensus* of exchange, production, capitalization, and distribution; (2) the extension of the use of this mathematical synthesis into economic dynamics where all of the variables in the constituent problems are treated as functions of time; and (3) the still further extension of this synthesis to the point of giving the equations concrete, statistical forms."[4]

This paper will address the issue of the reception and transformation of Léon Walras's work among some econometricians during the 1920s and 1930s. As will become obvious, the reception of Walras among the early econometricians has been as diverse as the work of these econometricians themselves. As set out below, the reception of Walras's work is related to the importance of the role of statistics, the dynamic representations of a changing reality and the consistency of simultaneous equations modelling.

The main contribution of this article lies perhaps in detecting these (different) reasons 'what went wrong with Walras' but should also be seen in the light of an extrapolated discussion of the current relevance of Léon Walras's work and his legacy for modern political economy.

The conclusion is that the reception of Walras by the early econometricians (statisticians and mathematicians together) was lukewarm, partly because it represented the wrong ideas and partly because of ignorance. When and where Walras's work was discussed it was mainly as a starting point to illustrate the relevance of the changes suggested by the newly founded econometric discipline. At then end of the day, this may illustrate the development of the economic discipline, but perhaps even more it may reveal the need for weaving Walras's applied and social economics into our present-day Walrasian texture.

2. STATISTICAL FORMS

The Econometric Society was founded in 1930, at the initiative of Irving Fisher and Ragnar Frisch. According to its constitution "its main object shall be to promote studies that aim at a unification of the theoretical-quantitative and empirical-quantitative approach to economic problems and that are penetrated by constructive and rigorous thinking similar to that which has come to dominate in the natural sciences."

As indicated by Ménard (1980), Walras's 'resistance' to statistics would not have made him an obvious fellow of the Econometric Society: the *Eléments d'économie politique pure* (1874) conveyed little sympathy towards empirical estimation or verification of his mathematical model. For the econometric pioneers of the Econometric Society there was consequently little in Walras's work to adhere to. Yet it is remarkable that whereas Walras was neglected by almost the entire econometric movement, A.-A. Cournot was heralded as the source of inspiration by many. In the econometric studies that made references to Walras and Cournot, the perceived difference between Walras and Cournot was, in part, based on the relation between theory and statistics. Cournot was perceived to allow for statistical estimation and/or verification of demand and supply relations, at least in principle, whereas Walras's deductive methodology would be hostile to numerical exposure. Although the former claim may be justified, for the latter it would seem too hastily to conclude that there would be no liaison possible between Walrasian theory and statistics. The following shreds of evidence may substantiate this point.

In 1874, in a letter to Cournot, Walras made his position towards statistics transparant:

> Our method is the same, because my method is yours. Only, you put yourself immediately in the position to benefit from the Law of Large Numbers and on the road that leads to numerical applications; as for myself, I do not go beyond this law while staying in the field of rigorous givens and of pure theory. But once my analysis is done I join you, and from that point I only have to follow you.[5]

In the Walrasian world the primacy of the mathematical model over reality is founded on the philosophical believes of its creator. In Walras's philosophy sciences study universals rather than particular instantiations. Statistics are particular instantiations and hence only relevant once the theoretical edifice has been constructed.[6] The method proclaimed by Walras not only establishes a relationship between economic theory and statistics but also established a sequence, and perhaps a hierarchy, between the two. He specified this in a letter to Bortkiewicz a quarter of a century later:

> Statistics is a discipline which may be illuminated by mathematical economics in many respects ...[7]

This implied for Walras that statistics only obtained meaning through the variables of the theory. Statistics, in this line of reasoning, had no heuristic value. The organisation of statistics would require the systematic classification of concepts and the principles of their behaviour:

> How, for instance, to organise the statistics of prices without a rational classification of prices and without the scientific knowledge of the principles of their realisation and their changes? That is impossible.[8]

3. SIMULTANEOUS EQUATIONS

Along mathematical lines Walras's model of general economic equilibrium was an impressive achievement, even though it remained enigmatic regarding the question where the system actually had an equilibrium solution. For some time, Walras's solution, equating the variables and equations as an indication for an equilibrium, served as a rule of thumb. With the development of mathematical economics also the issue of existence of an equilibrium solution popped up now and then. One of the early proofs came through the Vienna Circle meetings in the 1930s and deserves mentioning here.

After a long hibernation Walras's general economic equilibrium theory reemerged surprisingly in 1918 in Gustav Cassel's *Theory of Social Economy*, hence the references to the "Walras-Cassel" model from then on. In the 1930s the Walras-Cassel model was embraced whole-heartedly by the "Vienna Colloquium", run by the mathematician Karl Menger. Among the other participants in the Colloquium were Oskar Morgenstern, John von Neumann, Karl Schlesinger, and Abraham Wald.

The proceedings of the Colloquium[9] clearly illustrate traces of the logical positivist philosophy of the Vienna Circle, the mathematics of Hilbert's "formalist" programme and an occasional excursion to (Walrasian) general equilibrium theory.

The obvious instance of the embrace of the Walras-Cassel model within the Colloquium was the March 1934 session in which Schlesinger suggested a modification of the Walras-Cassel model in order to prove the existence of a general equilibrium. At the same session of the Colloquium Wald provided the first mathematical proof of the existence, which led Menger to conclude:

> In any case I would like to conclude that Wald's work seems to wind up a period in which economists have simply drawn up equations without taking care of the existence and unicity of their solution, and at best have observed the equality of variables and equations (which is of course neither necessary nor sufficient for existence and unicity of solutions). [10]

The reception of Walras's model by the Vienna Colloquium was above all 'warm' because of the mathematical problem that had existed since 1874 and that presented itself to be solved. Despite Menger accusation of sloppiness among economists the Walras-Cassel model opened a new venue for mathematical economists. With Von Neumann's 1932/37 article "A Model of General Equilibrium" general equilibrium theory was reduced to a bare minimum: a mathematical solution. As Debreu would later recall:

> The uncompromising precision of existence proofs forced on the Walrasian model an extensive reformulation that provided a framework for the research that occurred in several directions in GE theory. Knowing that the central concept of Walrasian theory existed under mild assumptions validated this research. [11]

The Von Neumann translation of "a typical economic system of equations" [12] into a generalisation of Brouwer's fixed point theorem takes Walrasian theory, however, a long way from home: in Von Neumann's article the mathematics has a phenomenological value incomparable to the function of Walras's mathematics. As set out by Von Neumann:

> A direct interpretation of the presented function $\Phi(X, Y)$ would very desirable. Its role seems to be similar to the one of thermodynamic potentials in the phenomenological thermodynamics. It is to be expected that it will also receive a similar role in full phenomenological generality (independent of our artificial restrictive idealisation.) [13]

Von Neumann's interpretation of the mathematics involved in his own work set the pace for later work in GE theory, but by doing so, the umbilical cord connecting the 19th and 20th century Walrasian theory was cut, never to be recuperated.

4. ECONOMIC DYNAMICS

As the econometric movement shifted into the direction of economic dynamics or dynamic economics, very few references to Walras's work were made. The obvious reason was the interest among the early econometricians in different phenomena and in different sorts of theories. As summarized by Jan Tinbergen in the early years of the Econometric Society:

> According to the definition of Frisch, the distinction between statics and dynamics is not a distinction between two sorts of phenomena, but a distinction between two sorts of theories, i.e. between two ways of thinking. The phenomena may be *stationary* or *changing*, the theory (the analysis) may be *static* or *dynamic*.[14]

Walras's theory was clearly perceived to be dealing with phenomena classified among the former category, despite Walras's cursorily treatment of a progressive society in the *Eléments,* whereas the interests of the econometric pioneers had shifted toward the second type of phenomena.

Another reason for the neglect of Walras's work was the static nature of the general equilibrium model itself. This is not to say that no attempt had been made to dynamize Walras, as the work by Charles Roos[15] and Henry Moore illustrate. In his 1927-paper (A dynamic theory of economic equilibrium) Charles Roos made an explicit attempt to produce "a dynamic generalization of the static theory of economic equilibrium of Walras and Pareto."[16] But rather than a dynamic generalization of Walras's static general equilibrium model, Roos analysed the mathematical requirements for the concept of maximum profit over an interval of time, for two types of economic settings: a competitive setting, in which producers consider the rates of production of competitors as fixed, and a cooperative setting in which the they are not fixed. Roos's analyses are, by definition, departures from Walras work, and its success in terms of econometric advance, is hard to estimate. As indicated by Roos:

> The theory as given in this paper is capable of quantitative verification for special simple problems. It is important to notice, however, that producers can hardly be expected to solve such a difficult problem by a cut-and-try method and obtain the correct solution. We should not therefore expect too close an agreement between theory and observations.[17]

Also Roos's later work, such as *Dynamic Economics* in 1934, failed dramatically to represent Walrasian economics in terms of economic dynamics, or perhaps even failed in general.

The second, odd, example is H.L. Moore, a one-time admirer of Walras and engraved in history as the crank who believed the causes of business cycles were found in the movements of the planet Venus.[18] Moore's estimation of demand and supply curves led him to formulate in 1925 so-called moving equilibria of demand and supply. The concept implied a reformulation of supply and demand by matching prices and quantities of two consecutive years, suggesting a dynamic concept. The concept of a moving equilibrium was brought in contact with Walras's model of simultaneous equations in Moore's *Synthetic Economics* (1929). In boasting terms he claimed that

> No mathematical economist, as far as I am aware, has ever attempted to pass from this or any similar presentation of a statical, hypothetical equilibrium to a realistic treatment of an actual, moving general equilibrium.[19]

Rather courageously, Moore replaced Walras's hypothetical demand and supply equations by his own moving equilibria of supply and demand; similar operations were performed on production, capitalization, credit etc. The attempt to make Walras's model dynamic was to adopt Moore's synthetic view and abandon Walrasian theory altogether:

> The method of the *Ecole de Lausanne* was to start with an unreal axiom: "la libre concurrence absolue"; to postulate a static state; and to adopt a convention with regard to equilibrium, which constituted a general balance of forces in the static state, "sous un regime hypothétique de libre concurrence absolue." The synthetic economist changes the convention, the postulate, and the axiom: His conventional equilibrium is the general equilibrium which economic forces actually at work in our perpetually changing economy tend to bring about; he postulates that this equilibrium tends to occur along the lines of general trend of the varying economic factors; he abandons the axiom of "la libre concurrence absolue" in favor of the Aristotelian matter of fact that business men go in the direction in which "the greatest profit can be made." Starting with the new convention, postulate, and axiom, he inquires what the conditions are that determine the moving equilibrium.[20]

Henry Moore found some response from Roos and Evans but in the end the caravan with leading econometricians such as Frisch or Tinbergen moved along developing their own concept of dynamic economics, without reference to Walras.

5. TAKE TINBERGEN

It should be acknowledged that Walrasian theory had largely paved the way for the development of econometrics and mathematical economics. Although the statisticians among the econometricians would largely object to the subsidiary role attributed to statistics by Walras, by and large most of these early econometricians would underline the dominance of theory. As, for instance, Tinbergen specified in his methodology of econometrics:

> The method essentially starts with *a priori* considerations about what explanatory variables are to be included. This choice must be based on economic theory or common sense.[21]

The continuation of the method, however, was empirical estimation of the variables, searching for reality rather than for universals.

Similarly, one might argue that the Walrasian proof of the existence of an equilibrium solution to a system of simultaneous equations was far from sophisticated, but most mathematical economists of the day could possibly agree with this general equilibrium research agenda on the table.

Perhaps the main problem in the 1920s and 1930s with Walras's theory was what it did *not* represent: reality. Although the arguments of the early econometricians may have differed in various ways, taking one particular story, i.e. Jan Tinbergen's, may illustrate the point.

Tinbergen's perception in 1926 that changing social and economic relations in society should have its repercussions on economic theory, had its immediate effect on the estimation of Walras's system of simultaneous equations. The point at stake was that Walras's model was perceived by Tinbergen to represent a situation of free competition and did not represent the actual economic situation anymore, if it ever did. In short: the system of equations did not model reality and were as such simply unacceptable for Tinbergen:

> Our society is full of sundry monopolies and half-monopolies, which in fact make the exchange equations of Walras unacceptable.[22]

The socialist debate on the organisation of production, and the related socialisation of production, led Tinbergen to search for economic literature on monopoly, oligopoly, cartels and trusts, and competition. In a rather courageous statement he claimed that despite the importance of competition in a capitalist society, it had been studied only superficially, with references to Böhm-Bawerk, Gide, Walras and Jevons. The only exception Tinbergen had encountered was A.A. Cournot:

> The only one who has studied the mechanism of competition and its quantitative effects more thoroughly than usual is A.A. Cournot in his 'Recherches sur les mathématiques de la Théorie des Richesses' which are, mind you, of 1838.[23]

In this line of search it was relevant that Cournot represented competition in terms of a series of extensions from monopoly (one supplier) to duopoly (two supplier) up to n suppliers. The approach seemed to suit Tinbergen's attitude towards science, stating the simplest case first and subsequently extending the case to more complex cases. The approach also suited Tinbergen's focus on the socialisation debate as it illustrated that free competition and oligopoly would transform naturally through the manipulation of the amount of suppliers.

In *Opmerkingen over Ruiltheorie*[24] (Observations on exchange theory) he stressed, that market equilibrium is not unequivocal in an isolated exchange situation and that further explanatory factors are required. Tinbergen argued that the "organisation of exchange" could be such an explanatory factor. With "organisation of exchange" he not only anticipated theories of different types of market structures but also argued that the meaning of 'exchange' would differ in each organisation of exchange. This implied that 'exchange' in a situation where prices are given to all participants would be of a different nature than 'exchange' where, e.g., one producer sets prices. Tinbergen further claimed that the 'usual' organisation of exchange, i.e. in which prices cannot be influenced by individuals, is not in line with daily experience and facts:

> The application of a solution [i.e. in which prices cannot be influenced by individuals] is not acceptable in every case, which is increasingly important for the economy, as the amount of monopolies and half-monopolies grows due to the increasing concentration.[25]

But even when the factual "organisation of exchange" was known then the solution would still remain wanting. The question at stake would be: what would be the equilibrium solution in a situation with relative few sellers and many buyers, in which the sellers set their prices, in competition, and in which the buyers take the price as given and determine demand accordingly.

> It should be noted that a solution to this question could hardly be found without mathematics. The only person – to my knowledge – who has given a solution is the mathematical economist Cournot.[26]

One of the type of questions Cournot's solution seemed to address was the influence of the process of increasing/decreasing competition, which Tinbergen observed in reality. The flux in cartelisation described by Hilferding's *Finance Capital*, was recognized by Tinbergen as a possible extension of Cournot's theory. In particular Cournot's theory could explain the behaviour of enterprises of differing 'organic composition of capital'[27] by assuming differing cost structures.

> Cournot's results can be extended and applied in different ways... Some peculiarities on the merging and demerging of cartels in peaks and slumps of the business cycle – as e.g. described by R. Hilferding in "Das Finanzkapital" – can be deduced from these exchange equations... This approach will in most cases be sufficiently precise and explain the differing behaviours of companies with differing "organische Zusammensetzung".[28]

Having read Rudolf Hilferding's '*Das Finanzkapital*' Tinbergen was convinced that a thorough study of the dynamics of the economic change in society should be given priority. Hilferding, who had become an influential social-democratic in Germany in the first quarter of the 20th century, described and analysed the "latest phase of capitalist development" and his book was perceived as a continuation of Marx's *Capital*. Tinbergen was struck by Hilferding's analysis of capitalism that predicted an increasing amount of trusts and cartels and increasing obstacles to free competition. Hilferding's work was also a far cry from the clean Walrasian world of free competition. With the "organization principle" as an important reason to denounce Walrasian theory, Tinbergen concluded:

> It seems to me a real advance in our understanding of problems concerning markets with few sellers that we now realize that for a solution of those problems, *there ought to be known more than the buyers' demand and the sellers' profit functions*, and, in addition, that there may be *several types of markets* ...[29]

This position was maintained in the annual *Econometrica* survey of 1934 where Walrasian theory was taken by Tinbergen as a starting point for discussion but only to illustrate that 'modern times' had led to refinements of, and deviation from, the Walrasian assumptions in order to model reality.

6. CONCLUSION

During the first quarter of the 20th Century economics has experienced a statistical turn: a new generation of economists were to bring theory closer to reality, to put existing theory to the test and to take the analysis to the dynamic domain. During the same period economics has also undergone a logico-mathematical reformulation leading a more disciplined transition of the mathematical foundations of economics.

The reception of Walras by the early econometricians (statisticians and mathematicians together) was lukewarm, partly because it represented the wrong ideas and partly because of ignorance. When and where Walras's work was discussed it was mainly as a starting point to illustrate the relevance of the changes suggested by the newly founded econometric discipline.

The current relevance of Walras's work, in connection to the econometric reception in the 1920s and 1930s, is to answer the question 'What went wrong with Walras?' In the above this question has been addressed. What remains are the unanswered questions about the relations between theory and empirical reality. The econometric achievements of the last 50 years suggest a re-examination of this question. This may well imply that Walras's system of simultaneous equations will require further study as to its embeddedness in an institutional environment. For this a better understanding of Walras's applied economics and social economics is required, as Blaug (2001) has argued. Only then will Walras contribute to the future development of the discipline.

NOTES

1. Moore to Walras, 10 April 1908, L.1685 in: Walras (1965).
2. Morgan (1990), p. 5.
3. See, e.g., Ingrao and Israel (1987).
4. Moore (1929), p. 6.
5. Walras to Cournot, 20 March 1874, L.352 in Walras (1965).
6. See also Jolink (1996).
7. Walras to Bortkiewics, 30 July 1899, L. 1415 in Walras (1965).
8. Walras to Bortkiewicz, 9 January 1891, L. 996 in Walras (1965).
9. Published as *Ergebnisse eines mathematischen Kolloquiums*.
10. "Jedenfalls möchte ich zum Schluss bemerken, dass mir mit der Waldschen Arbeit die Periode abgeschlossen erscheint, in der die Ökonomen Gleichungen bloss *aufgestellt* haben, ohne sich um Existenz und Eindeutigkeit ihrer Lösungen zu kümmern, und bestenfalls darauf sahen, dass die Anzahl der Unbekannten mit der Anzahl der Gleichungen übereinstimme (was für Existenz und Unizität von Lösungen natürlich weder notwendig noch hinreichend ist)." Menger (1998), p. 290.
11. G. Debreu, 'Economics in a Mathematics Colloquium', in Menger (1998), p. 4.

12. Von Neumann in Menger (1998), p. 453.
13. Von Neumann in Menger (1998), p. 453-454. Note that notion of the role of functions is similar to Tinbergen's application of thermodynamics to economics in Tinbergen (1929).
14. Tinbergen (1934), p. 26-27.
15. Charles Roos was one of the founders of the Econometric Society and became research director of the Cowles Commission in 1934.
16. Roos (1927), p. 280.
17. Roos (1927a), p. 655.
18. See, e.g., Morgan (1990), p. 26-30.
19. Moore (1929), p. 106.
20. Moore (1929), p. 181-182.
21. Tinbergen (1939), p. 10.
22. Tinbergen (1926).
23. Tinbergen (1925).
24. Tinbergen (1928).
25. Tinbergen (1928).
26. Id. p. 440-441.
27. Hilferding's term.
28. Tinbergen (1928).
29. Tinbergen (1934), p. 16.

REFERENCES

Blaug, M. (2001). "No history of ideas, please, we're economists", *Journal of Economic Perspectives*, 15, 1, 145-164.
Hilferding, R. (1981). *Finance Capital*, London: Routledge & Kegan Paul.
Ingrao, B. and Israel, G. (1987). *The Invisible Hand: Economic Equilibrium in the History of Science*, Cambridge, Mass.: MIT Press.
Jolink, A. (1996). *The Evolutionist Economics of Léon Walras*, London: Routledge.
Ménard, C. (1980). "Three forms of resistance to statistics: Say, Cournot, Walras", *History of Political Economy*, 12, 4, 524-541.
Menger, K. (1998). *Ergebnisse eines Mathematischen Kolloquiums*, edited by E. Dierker and K. Sigmund, Wien: Springer.
Moore, H.L. (1911). *Laws of Wages: An essay in Statistical Economics*, New York: Macmillan.
Moore, H.L. (1925). "A moving equilibrium of demand and supply", *Quarterly Journal of Economics*, May, 357-371.
Moore, H.L. (1929). *Synthetic Economics*, New York: Macmillan.
Morgan, M. (1990). *The History of Econometric Ideas*, Cambridge: CUP.
Roos, C.F. (1927). "A dynamical theory of economic equilibrium", *Proceedings of the National Academy of Sciences of the USA*, 13, 5, 280-285.
Roos, C.F. (1927a), "A dynamical theory of economic equilibrium", *Journal of Political Economy*, 35, 637-656.
Tinbergen, J. (1925). "Opmerkingen over konkurrentie", *Kentering*, (1), 7/8.
Tinbergen, J. (1926). "Opmerkingen over de arbeidswarde", *Kentering*, (2) 2.

Tinbergen, J. (1928). "Opmerkingen over Ruiltheorie", *De Socialistische Gids*, 13, 431-445 and 539-548.
Tinbergen, J. (1929). *Minimumproblemen in de natuurkunde en de ekonomie*, Amsterdam: H.J. Paris.
Tinbergen, J. (1934). "Annual survey of significant developments in general economic theory", *Econometrica*, 2, 13-36.
Tinbergen, J. (1939). *Statistical Testing of Business-cycle Theories: Business Cycles in the United States of America 1919-1932*, Geneva: League of Nations Publications.
Walras, L. (1965). *Correspondence of Léon Walras and Related Papers*, edited by W. Jaffé, Amsterdam: North-Holland.

PART II

Vilfredo Pareto

7. Vilfredo Pareto and Public Choice: A Reappraisal

Helge Peukert

University of Erfurt, Germany

Abstract In this short recapitulation of Pareto's theory of residues we wanted to present their basic elements and give examples in how far they may help explain non-logical actions which cannot be explained by sophisticated information cost arguments. It may be repeated that Pareto argues in an evolutionary, Darwinian way. Behind the residues are sentiments and drives which were more or less functional in the development of the human species and which have strong corollaries in animal behavior. From a logical point of view, many of these residues are non-functional today but they help understand many occurrences in the real world which are beyond the capabilities of rational man or rational choice explanations.

Keywords: Darwin, Pareto's Theory of Residues, Public Choice, Schumpeter

JEL classification: B13, B25

1. PARETO AND PUBLIC CHOICE

"In his *Trattato di Sociologia Generale* (1916), Vilfredo Pareto outlined a generalised theory of social interaction which methodologically is the application of economic reasoning to the analysis of not only the economy, but also of a conceptually enlarged system" (Backhaus, 1999/1978, p. 395). Pareto's sociological opus magnum which was translated in 1935 into English as *Mind and Society* (Pareto, 1963) has received great attention among social scientists since its first publication.[1] It would not be surprising that economists who like to broaden the horizon of economic analysis, e.g. in the context of new institutional economics had a closer lock at the almost 2000 pages of Pareto's *Trattato*. But, in fact, "(e)conomists tend either to ignore or to neglect Pareto's *comprehensive* approach which, unlike the purely economic general equilibrium theory, has always been alien to them" (Backhaus, 1999, p. 395).

Backhaus points out that it is especially surprising that the parallels between public choice theory and Pareto's oeuvre have not been recognized. We find e.g. the following sentence in Pareto's *Trattato*: "A politician is inspired to champion the theory of "solidarity" by an ambition to obtain money, power, distinctions. Analysis of that theory would reveal but scant trace of his motives, which are, after all, the motives of virtually all politicians, whether they preach white or black" (1963, p. 502, §854). This is in exact conformity with the traditional public choice approach developed by Downs, Buchanan and Tullock (see the overview in Tullock, 1998). They view politicians as acting not primarily in the public interest but for their own well-being. Other central points in public choice are that voters are seen as customers and politicians as businessmen or entrepreneurs which favor topics which they do not think are right but which allows them to be re-elected. Voters, politicians and bureaucracies are assumed to be motivated by self-interest.

"Basically the average employee in a bureaucracy is interested in retaining his job and gaining promotion and for this purpose wants to please his superiors" (Tullock, 1998, p. 1042). In this view, voters are extremely ignorant about politics in general because of their lack of influence and they are mainly informed about those special interests which include strong pecuniary effects. Ideologies have a rational component insofar as they are a cheap short-cut of basic orientations. Politicians vote "and seek public positions in terms of what they think the voters *will* reward, not in terms of what they think the *voters* should reward" (Tullock, 1998, p. 1041).

Interestingly, "(t)here is even no reference to Pareto's *Treatise* in Gordon Tullock's Appendix (2) on "Theoretical Forerunners" to the *Calculus of Consent*" (Backhaus, 1999, p. 405, fn. 11). The reason may be that at a closer look Pareto fundamentally deviates from the public choice frame of reference. Backhaus points out a main conceptual difference when he asserts that "ignoring the cost of gathering and processing information, Pareto insisted on logical action as the only adequate justified action.... Objectively, most non-logical action will be *rational* behaviour in the economic sense, if the costs of information and the individual costs of transgressing social normation are taken into account" (1999, pp. 397 and 405, fn. 14). In Downs analysis (1957), ideological commitments (derivations) are not rationalizations of deep-seated non-rational sentiments (residues) as in Pareto but they are viewed as rational individual behavior because it relates means to ends under informational cost restrictions. For Downs, the politician is seen as an ideology engineering entrepreneur who cool-hearted delivers the script for the mostly disinterested rational customers. For Pareto, ideologies or derivations reflect man's "desire to logicalize conduct that is non-logical" (1963, p. 770, §1275). Pareto's citation from above on the politician continues consequently: "Oftentimes the person who would persuade others [the politician] begins by persuading himself.... Unbelieving apostles are rare and ineffective, but ubiquitous and ubiquitously effective is the apostle who believes, and he is the more effective, the more sincere his belief. The element *a* [residues] in a theory *c* is present both in the persons who accept and in the persons who propound it" (1963, pp. 502-503, §854).

To state major differences in the theoretical basic orientations between Pareto and public choice (Downs, Tullock, Buchanan) is not to say that no links and no complementary relations exist between Pareto and economists which are considered as relevant heretics in the public choice camp. In the last years some authors pointed out that Schumpeter was only in a very limited sense a precursor of public choice. Instead his approach is considered as a corrective approach against a certain one-sidedness of certain public choice assumptions on the political process (Mitchell, 1984; Prisching, 1995; Wohlgemuth, 2001). Nevertheless, also the strong affinity between public choice and Schumpeterian political economy should be kept in mind, i.e. their – and Pareto's – rejection of the assumptions that people act for the common good and that democratic governments maximize welfare. After shortly delineating Schumpeter's major peculiarities we will develop the thesis that Schumpeter's and Pareto's framework supplement each other and also point out some differences.

2. THE SCHUMPETERIAN POLITICAL ECONOMY

Schumpeter develops his alternative concept mainly in his *Capitalism, socialism and democracy* (1996/1942). He observes that "the typical citizen drops down to a lower level of mental performance as soon as he enters the political field He argues and analyzes in a way which he would readily recognize as infantile within the sphere of his real interests. He becomes a primitive again. His thinking becomes associative and affective" (1996, p. 262). Successful politicians do not only aggregate interests of the electorate, they manage emotions, for example "sentiments of belonging to a party, feelings of national pride, expressions of shame over military defeat and so on ... [For Schumpeter], (i)nformation is shaped by political ideology and intellectual fashion, by public sentiment and pseudo-science" (Prisching, 1995, pp. 306-307).

As we will shortly see, these examples coincide with some major Paretian residues. Schumpeter and Pareto share the view – contrary to public choice – that irrationalities dominate the political process. In fact, Downs (1957, p. 29, fn. 11) explicitly mentions Schumpeter as a precursor, so that we find the Schumpeter-Downs theory of democracy in the literature (Udehn, 1996, p. 18), but in the whole book Schumpeter is only mentioned twice and in insignificant respects. The affective side is emphasized by Schumpeter again and again. "Every parliament, every committee ..., displays, in however mild a form, some of those features that stand out so glaringly in the case of the rabble, in particular a reduced sense of responsibility, a lower level of energy of thought and greater sensitiveness to non-logical influences" (1996, p. 257). In his description of the emotional voting process Schumpeter also refers to Pareto besides e.g. Freud and Le Bon. As Backhaus observed, in the essential chapters 22 and 23 of *Capitalism* which contain the outline of Schumpeter's alternative theory of democracy, there is not a single reference to Pareto (1999, p. 405, fn. 11).

Schumpeter voters do not have consistent and stable preferences and to a large degree they are unable to assess their objective interests which contradicts the public choice median voter model. "It might be possible for political incumbents to respond to public pressure not by fulfilling demands but by reducing them through "moral suasion," e.g., by appealing to a state of national emergency to awaken nationalist sentiments ... politics does not only deal with fulfilling voter preferences. Changing the preferences and even identities of citizens is an integral part of real-world political strategies" (Prisching, 1995, p. 303). This is the major task for the political entrepreneur. In so far, "the will of the people is the product and not the motive power of the political process" (Schumpeter, 1996, p. 263).

Schumpeter refers in his general image of entrepreneurship to Nietzsche, Bergson, Sombart and Wieser. As Schumpeter developed in his *The theory of economic development* (1952/1912), entrepreneurs are driven by strong impulses like founding an empire, etc. "According to Schumpeter, he who has nothing to provide but rationality cannot be an entrepreneur. Entrepreneurial rationality is not the uniform rationality beloved by rational choice theorists" (Prisching, 1995, p. 308; compare again Pareto, 1963, §843). "Collectives act almost exclusively by accepting leadership" (Schumpeter, 1996, p. 270).

Consequently, Schumpeter defines democracy as "that institutional arrangement for arriving at political decisions in which individuals acquire the power to decide by means of a competitive struggle for the people's vote" (1996, p. 269). To differentiate Schumpeter from public choice Prisching calls Schumpeter's approach an irrational choice theory which is a deliberate contradiction in terms to point out the peculiar combination of rational and irrational influences in the political process.

We may summarize with Wohlgemuth that "by attaching high standards of rationality to political actors, by treating political issues and preferences as given and by modelling political competition as a state in which politicians passively adapt to any given majority will, much of Public Choice largely remains within rationalistic and idealistic traditions ... [it can be shown] that both major elements in Schumpeter's account: citizens' irrationality and politicians' leadership are not only ignored but even turned to their almost complete opposites" (2001, pp. 3, and 1). To cite Schumpeter again: "There is no such thing as a universal pattern of rationality" (1996, p. 258, fn. 10). In the next part we will analyze, if Pareto shared the irrational choice paradigm (for a critique of rational choice from a non-autocratic point of view see Kuttner, 1998, pp. 333ff.).

3. IS PARETO'S SOCIOLOGY AN IRRATIONAL CHOICE THEORY?

Pareto's ideal for sociological analysis are the natural sciences. "(M)y wish is to construct a system of sociology on the model of celestial mechanics, physics, chemistry" (1963, p. 16, §20). Therefore, he distinguishes sharply logical form non-logical actions. Logical actions are those which "logically conjoin means to ends not only from the standpoint of the subject performing them, but from the standpoint of other persons who have a more extensive knowledge – in other words, to actions that are logical both subjectively and objectively in the sense just explained. Other actions we shall call *non-logical*" (1963, p. 77, §150). To be logical, ends must be the result of reasoning and they must be in the fields of observation and experience. The Greek mariners who sacrifice to Poseidon and who are rowing with oars are for our best knowledge using non-logical actions for navigation. Actions are non-logical insofar as (1) the real efficacy of the means is not verifiable, or which are (2) objectively not efficacious means to the ends, or which are (3) not done as reasoned means to an end, or (4) actions which are not done as reasoned means to an end but which do serve as an end (1963, p. 78, §151). The first two cases are the most important.

The next question is what the origin of these types of action are. In his analysis "(l)ogical actions are at least in large part results of processes of reasoning. Non-logical actions originate chiefly in definite psychic states, sentiments, subconscious feelings, and the like" (1963, pp. 87-88, §161). His strong thesis is that all non-logical actions are not result of reasoning but expressions of subconscious feelings. This thesis is compatible with Schumpeter's assumption of citizens irrationality, but not with public choice's rationalist assumption. Theories of nationalism, democracy etc. are primarily results of these feelings and simple rationalizations. Belief in democracy is only an expression of the religion of progress and not at all different from religious sectarian thinking. We see already, that Pareto attacks the view (like public choice and Schumpeter) that people and politicians act for the common good once they enter democratic decision making and that democratic governments will maximize welfare.

In a certain sense his methodological ideal, the precision of the natural sciences and the rejection of hermeneutical techniques or the method of *Verstehen,* comes close to the methodological ideal of public choice, but not of

Schumpeter. Tullock for example highlights the methodological rigor of public choice. "Public Choice is a new and radical approach to government, but its firm foundations in economic methodology mean that we have more confidence in its accuracy than most new ideas. Further, it has by now been empirically tested very thoroughly" (Tullock, 1998, p. 1044). The simple empiricism and positivism of Pareto has often been castigated not only by frank constructivists ("we have to appeal to observation and experience, which alone can yield trustworthy data", 1963, p. 336, §556). In fact, individuals and groups have to rely on common reference systems and shared values (Backhaus, 1999, p. 398, and Samules, 1974, p. 127).

People need a definition of the situation which has nothing to do with simple expressions of subconscious feelings. In a lucid analysis of Pareto's methodology, Macpherson shows that Pareto's thesis of the sentimental underlying of non-logical action is nowhere proven. "Much of people's conduct is, of course, the result of habit and custom, but where ultimate issues are in question, is there any more evidence for believing that people act directly from subconscious feelings and think up reasons afterwards to justify them, than for the other view that they act in what they think is the logical way to attain the end given by the subconscious feelings?" (1999/1937, p. 289). We may state that this assumption is Pareto's s unconscious feeling and residue. It is one-sided but an excellent counter-assumption to the rationality frame of public choice.

For Pareto, constructs of mind (like ideologies) which are non-logical are divided into two components: the residues and the derivations. "Residues correspond to certain instincts in human beings" (1963, p. 509, §870). They become manifest in human non-logical actions and in ideologies. Their pseudo-logical justifications are called derivations. "Human beings are persuaded in the main by sentiments (residues), and we may therefore foresee, as for that matter experience shows, that derivations derive the force they have, not ... from logico-experimental considerations, but from sentiments. The principal nucleus in a derivative (a non-logico-experimental theory) is a residue, or a number of residues, and around it other secondary residues cluster. That group is produced, and once, produced is consolidated, by a powerful force: the need that the human being feels for logical or pseudo-logical developments and which manifests itself in residues of the I-ε type" (1963, pp. 885-886, §1397).

Residues are anthropologically deep-seated constant elements, the derivations are variable, the same residue can be the underlay of many different derivations. Residues are the drivers of human conduct. We may state already, that according to this theoretical exposition, Prisching's paradoxical notion of irrational choice theory in which irrational and rational elements of action are interwoven (1995, p. 315, fn. 2) exactly fits Pareto's construction of residues, derivations (and interests, see below). Pareto's image of man is an in-between of logical and non-logical attitudes and actions. "Science can merely relate one fact to another. There is always, therefore, a fact at which it comes to a halt. The human imagination refuses to stop there. It insists on going on, insists on drawing inferences even from the ultimate fact, on knowing its "cause," and if it cannot find a real cause it invents an imaginary one" (1963, p. 591, §973).

It may be mentioned in passing that besides the residues a second major variable influences the structure and change in society and economy: the interests. They are defined as instincts which animate actors "to acquire possession of material goods that are useful – or merely pleasurable – for purposes of living, as well as to seek consideration and honours ... That mass of interests falls in very considerable part within the purview of the science of economics" (1963, p. 1406, §§2009-2010). The emphasis of interests is shared by Pareto and public choice. But for Pareto, non-interest residues are as important as interests. From a Paretian bias e.g. the rationality assumption of public choice is another expression of the religion of progress and a biased view of the real world. Pareto's view leads to an analysis of ideology critique when he states, "that the experimental "truth" of certain theories is one thing and their social "utility" quite another, and that the two things are not only not one and the same but may, and often do, stand in flat contradiction" (1963, p. 500, §843).

So Pareto is opposed to Downs' view of the rational voter for whom the "*vote value* is compounded from his estimates of his party differential and of the probability that his vote will be decisive" (1957, p. 244). Interestingly, Downs enlarges the motive set: "A rational man may buy political information because (1) he wishes to influence the government's policies, (2) his prediction of how other voters will act indicates that the probability is relatively high that his own vote will be decisive, or (3) he derives entertainment value or social prestige from such data" (1957, p. 245). In these passages, non-rational aspects are smuggled into the picture. "It is sometimes rational for a citizen to vote even when his short-run costs exceed his short-run returns, because social responsibility produces a long-run return" (1957, p. 261). Here, Downs is aware of other than clearly specified self-interested motives but he compressed them in his rationality framework. It is very doubtful, if he succeeded (see the criticism in Wohlgemuth, 2001, pp. 10ff.). In so far Pareto captures aspects of reality which are paradigmatic anathema for public choice.

Pareto distinguishes six classes of residues which will be discussed in more detail in the next section. Here we will only mention the most two important residues for his sociological theory: The instinct for combinations (I) and those of the persistence of aggregates (II). "Residue I consists of a desire to get ahead, a liking for experiment and for trying new things and new ways of doing things, a disposition always to take a chance, a quality of shrewdness, a preference for cunning rather than force, and an absorption in immediate tangible interests. Residue II consists in the spirit of conservatism, the desire to hold fast to established things and ways of doing things, a slow-moving mentality, a quality of courage and loyalty, a preference for force rather than cunning, and a greater reverence for ideal and transcendental ends than for the immediate interests of the individual" (Macpherson, 1999, p. 291).

Residue I was dominant in classical Athens and is dominant in speculator groups, residue II in Sparta and today in rentier groups. Pareto never quantifies or put his residues in a strict model, somewhat contrary to his methodological ideal. He also deviates from the principle of methodological individualism. "In individuals sentiments are always more or less complex, sometimes very much so. In making a scientific analysis, therefore, we have to fix our main attention on sentiments, not on individuals" (1963, p. 673, §1137). Residues may vary according to the stage of development and among social groups and strata. "The need of uniformity [e.g.] is much more strongly felt among uncivilized than among civilized peoples ... it may also differ according to the various groupings of individuals within the people" (1963, p. 660, §§115-116). It can also happen that in a whole population a residue class domination switch takes place due to extraordinary circumstances. In the following section we will take the reactions of the American people and government to the attacks at the World Trade Center on September 11 (2001) as our example. It was a surprising observation that after September 11 for almost two months a residue switch took place (not only) in New York, the city which most accurately represents the residue formation of class I and which turned to class II in the aftermath of the catastrophe for a while.

It is striking how close Pareto comes to evolutionary approaches in general and to Schumpeter's analysis in particular if we consider his two most important classes of residues. In a footnote, A. Livingston, the translator of *Mind and Society*, mentions that Pareto's instinct for combinations (residue class I) is more comprehensive in Italian (*combinazione*) than in English and in the respective context should be translated as happy inspiration, inventive faculty, ingeniousness, etc. If we also take into consideration the opposing instinct of group-persistence as the conservative force we detect a striking similarity with Schumpeter's distinction between statics and dynamics and his description of the abilities and functions of entrepreneurs. This especially holds if we consider the original chapter seven in the first edition of Schumpeter's *Theorie der wirtschaftlichen Entwicklung* (1912) in which he tried to apply the principles of statics and dynamics to society as a whole, in our view, a rather unsuccessful attempt (Peukert, 2002). Pareto's dynamic-static approach can also be found in Ch.S. Peirce and his distinction between spontaneous mutations and habit formations, who strongly influenced Veblen (Peukert, 1998, pp. 285-296). Veblen's idle curiosity corresponds to Pareto's residue I class, habit formations and preconceptions to Pareto's residue II class. In evolutionary terminology, class I is variation, class II stabilization. The entrepreneurs are the selective link between variation and selection, the transformation of inventions into innovations. It may be mentioned that Pareto often uses biological examples and Darwinian explanations and puts them in a sociobiological context. "If a hen is painted red and returned to its flock, the other hens at once attack it" (1963, p. 660, §1115). The same need of uniformity can be found in humans, as cited above.

In our view, Macpherson is correct to state that Pareto is really interested in one or two questions in his book: "What are the conditions for the successful domination of the many by the few? ... (W)hy do civilizations and empires and nations rise and fall?" (1999, p. 292). Schumpeter asks the same main questions in his *Capitalism* and he also shares Pareto's basic assumption: "Collectives act almost exclusively by accepting leadership" (Schumpeter, 1996, p. 270). The theory of class-circulation delivers Pareto's answer to these questions. For him there always exists a ruling and a subject class. The power of the ruling class and the stability of society depends on an adequate mixture of residues I and II in the ruling class (I: cunning, propaganda and manipulation plus II: the willingness to use force) and among all social classes. Usually, first residues II dominate to attain power and the formulation of ideals. But when society develops and the economy grows the shrewd and crafty will supplement the ruling class. When the ruling class is composed almost solely of residue I characters with intelligence and cunning but without the will to use force, an upheaval may take place. If the class-circulation is arbitrarily stopped by the ruling class a collapse may ensue. For Pareto, the major fight takes place between the strong lions and the cunning foxes, the rentiers and the speculators, the conservatives and the progressives. In Schumpeter, we find a different explanation of the breakdown of empires and capitalism: the disappearance of pre-capitalist modes of thinking and structures. The voting oscillation models in public choice also refer to different variables than Pareto's.

But the change of residues at different times and places is not random. It depends on the economic factor, i.e. logical action and "interests".[2] Growth and prosperity always alter the proportion of the residue classes in society, from class II to class I. So the economic factor plays a major role in the explanation of the composition of residues. Logical and non-logical action have equal importance for Pareto.

Macpherson finally holds that Pareto simply gave a new name to things that still need to be explained and he casts "grave doubts on the scientific validity and theoretical usefulness of Pareto's sociology" (1999, p. 295). In the next paragraph we will analyze Pareto's residues and derivations in more detail and ask if they are useful or not. The result of this section is that Pareto can be considered as a representative of an irrational choice theory and that a lot of similarities with Schumpeter came to the fore.

4. RESIDUES AND DERIVATIONS

Pareto distinguishes six classes of residues, all except one with subdivisions (§§888ff.; see the appendix with the complete list). The instinct for combinations has six main subdivisions. It "is an inclination to combine certain things with certain other things. The scientist in his laboratory ... His activity is primarily logical. The ignorant person makes combinations in view of analogies that are mostly fantastic, absurd, childish (and often also by chance). In any event they are in large part non-logical acts" (1963, p. 519, §889). Often they are fleeting and momentary, at least in the category of generic combinations (I-α), e.g. the choosing of birthday dates in lotteries. When similar or opposite things are combined we get genus I-β. It comprises the combining of unusual things with exceptional occurrences, but also assimilation in the sense of physical consumption of substances to get effects of associable or opposite character. In genus I-γ mysterious workings of things are listed, e.g. the mysterious linking of names and things and many rites of magic.

The three last genera of the instinct for combinations are first the need for combining residues (I-δ), i.e. "a synthetic tendency which is indispensable to practical life ... The human being is loath to dissever faith from experience; he wants a completed whole free from discordant notes" (1963, p. 588, §§966-967). Next is the need or hunger for logical development (I-ε). "At bottom what people want is to think – it matters little whether the thinking be sound or fallacious" (1963, p. 590, §972). Finally comes the faith in the efficacy of combinations (I-ζ). "Oftentimes he [man] is indifferent to experimental verifications. Often again, if he does give them a thought he rests content with utterly insufficient, sometimes even ridiculous, proofs" (1963, p. 592, §978).

We see that the instinct of combinations refers to pseudo-logical combinations of many sorts including superstition, ceremonial (Veblen) and low-level reasoning. Pareto has a fairly critical attitude vis-à-vis the first class of residues and as we shall see, against all residues. They do not seem to foster imagination and innovation at all but foreclose insight in the real world. We may ask, in how far this instinct is characteristic for the cunning and the speculator who to a certain extent dominate New York (before September 11, 2001), our prime example.

We may briefly refer here to some basic insights of behavioral finance to show equivalents to Pareto's residue class I in the mind set of those working at Wall Street(s). Behavioral finance is a branch of capital market analysis besides chartist and fundamental analysis. It focuses on emotions, mass psychology, the fact of informational overload, that many people may err in the same direction, and that they use questionable heuristics and – as Pareto called them – childish analogies to reduce complexity (Goldberg and Nitzsch, 2000). One result of behavioral finance is that even professionals at Wall Street are strongly influenced by heuristics of disposability: objective data are neglected instead of recent, new, loud and illustrative events, the fleeting and momentary in Pareto's words. The contrast effect also holds here: those impressions are relevant which mostly differ from the known environment (Pareto's unusual things and occurrences). Another striking parallel is the anchoring effect, i.e. the dependence of judgments on initial values and the conjunction fallacy which describes the fact that events which are not connected are regarded as connected and those which are connected are regarded as disconnected (Goldberg and Nitzsch, 2000, pp. 73ff.). These facts correspond to Pareto's combination of similars and opposites. This fallacy is often combined with the conditional probability fallacy, i.e. the mix-up of cause and effect.

Very often economic agents exaggerate empirical connections. For example, for some time almost all firms listed at the *Neuer Markt* in Germany experienced increasing stock prices because they were regarded in conjunction with other successful *Neuer Markt* firms which corrsponds to Pareto's mysterious linkings. We will further mention the observation in behavioral finance that many people are closed minded consistency seekers, they try to evade information and situations which contradict their habitual mind combinations (Goldberg and Nitzsch, 2000, pp. 111ff.), in Pareto's words: they want to be free form discordant notes (Festinger's theoy of cognitive dissonance may also be mentioned in this context). Finally we will only note the need for the control of the environment, people at least invent retrospectively illusions of explanations why things had to happen the way they happened which corresponds to Pareto's residues hunger for logical development, efficacy of combinations and the belief in pseudo-proofs. Pareto's approach could also be used to transcend the rather simplistic archaic models of man in behavioral finance (e.g. the thesis of the threefold reptile brain, see Goldberg and Nitzsch, 2000, pp. 163ff.). Here we will only emphasize the parallel that in behavioral finance and in Pareto's understanding the operations of the brain are a composite of instincts, emotions (residues) and reason (derivations).

The second main class of residues is the persistence of aggregates, or simply group persistences with eight subdivisions. It contains groups of aggregates or associations of sensations that the human mind confirms into units that persist in time, become habitual or customary. Further, names are ascribed to them which lead to personifications like "God," "Russia," or "Uncle Sam." An example is that a people selects a river as their god. "After the group has been constituted, an instinct very often comes into play that tends with varying energy to prevent the things so combined from being disjoined ...

This instinct may be compared roughly to mechanical inertia: it tends to resist the movement imparted by other instincts. To that fact the tremendous social importance of Class II residues is to be ascribed" (1963, p. 598, §992). Genus II-α comprises the persistence of relations between a person and other persons and places. It is a permanent sentiment attaching people to other people and places and constitutes a certain sense of spatial property which can also be observed in animals. We will only mention the subgroup relations with places and omit those of family and kindred group and relationships of social class. "Something similar takes place among modern peoples. Looking at things superficially, one might imagine that patriotism of the modern type is a matter of territory ... But looking a little more closely, one perceives that in awakening sentiments of patriotism the territorial name suggests a sum of sentiments, language, religion, traditions, history, and so on" (1963, p. 622, §1042).

The reaction of the American people to September 11 as a threatening experience was an overwhelming patriotism and a reaffirmation of group persistences. In case of a disturbance of social equilibrium, the residual forces of inertia are set in motion. In our example, even shopping became a quasi-metaphysical duty in the war against terrorism. Stars-and-stripes bras, liberty barbies and red-white-blue M&Ms are also part of the war. It was surprising how strongly the majority of New Yorkers confirmed their relations with places who on average have a rather instrumental and cool-blooded relationship to their town. We could also observe the quasi-religious reference to the spirit of the town and its history, etc. Genus II-β refers to the persistence of relations between the living and the dead. They "appear in such complex phenomena as honouring or worshipping the dead, or banquets and sacrifices connected with funerals or commemorations" (1963, p. 629, §1052). The commemoration e.g. in the Yankee Stadium is an impressive example of this residue which normally includes the belief in the immortality of the soul. It seems to us that these reactions cannot be explained in a rationalist way, e.g. with reference to information costs or the reduction of transaction costs by common frames of interpretation. A rational reaction would consist in the citizen's indifference and an attitude of 'make the pecuniary best of the situation.'

We only mention the groups II-δ, the persistence of abstractions (persistence of theologies and metaphysical systems as a powerful social force), II-ε, the persistence of uniformities (a fact is stated in abstract language and becomes a general rule), II-ζ, the sentiments transformed into objective realities (Freud's projection), II-θ, the need of new abstractions, and II-η, personifications (anthropomorphism). The latter includes abstract and diffuse concepts like "liberty," "the free or democratic world," a rhetoric which plays a major role in the rhetorical battle in the war against terrorism ("socialism" would be another example). A personification can also consist in the identification of a person or a country ("Russia") as the universal bad.

Class III comprises the need of expressing sentiments by external acts, including religious ecstasies to escape from a state of passive abstraction. An example is a cat which moves its jaws at sight of a bird. "The impulse to "do something" is overwhelming; the fancy sets to work, and finds a way to satisfy it" (1963, p. 648, §1092). Many activities of New Yorkers after September 11 may be subsumed under this category, e.g. many helping activities which hardly made sense; this residue may also be partly active in the many ceremonial-religious meetings and celebrations.

Class IV residues (with six subsets) are those which are connected with sociality, including disciplinary residues. They are mostly disregarded in the secondary literature but in Pareto's and our view they are of major importance because they deal with essential aspects of life in society which can also be found among almost all animal species. Genus IV-α on particular societies means the need for particular associations of many different kinds, from mere amusement to political, religious and cultural purposes. It expresses the fact that man is a socializing animal. The next major genus is the need for conformity which is also strong in animals. One part is voluntary conformity on the part of the individual. Pareto has the phenomenon of imitation in mind which is manifest in e.g. fashion. The deliberate habit of Americans to buy goods with national symbols or to paint the national flag on the roof or the doors may be a recent example.

The second aspect is uniformity enforced upon others. "If a person departs from the uniform rule, his conduct seems to jar, and produces, quite apart from any reasoning, a sense of discomfort in the persons associated with him. An effort is made to eliminate the jar, now by persuasion, more often by censure, more often still by force. As usual, there is no lack of logical chatter to explain such procedures" (1963, p. 664, §1126). An expression of this tendency in the US is the intellectual surrender of the free press and the media. Major information channels like CNN continuously inserted a permanently waving national flag. Those who criticized the military strategy of permanent bombing of Afghanistan were severely criticized. Members of the R. Nader staff and the American green party were put on a list and airlines rejected them as customers. Genus β3 comprises neophobia, i.e. a hostility to innovations that would disturb uniformities.

The next genus is pity and cruelty. "Sentiments of pity at all intense are felt, chiefly, for people who stand before one's eyes" (1963, p. 671, §1134). Self-pity is often extended to others (genus γ1) who are regarded with a benevolent eye because they are assumed to suffer for the same reasons (we will leave out the residues of the repugnance of suffering). The next major genus is self-sacrifice for the good of others, the first subcategory is risking one's life. "Very beautiful theories have been evolved to show that a man *ought* to love his country. However, the effect of such theories is virtually nil. It is insignificant at any rate as compared with the influence of the non-logical sentiment that inspires patriotism ... People risk or even sacrifice their lives out of deep feelings of sociality" (1963, pp. 680-681, §1146, and 1148). The New York firefighters are the impressive example for this residue (we leave out the sub-genera sharing one's property with others and asceticism).

In the residues of sociality we find next the sentiments of social ranking or hierarchy. The sentiments of superiors "are sentiments of patronage and benevolence, supplemented oftentimes by domineering sentiments, or sentiments of pride" (1963, pp. 686-687, §1155). The former mayor of New York expressed these sentiments while the American president had to learn how to express them. The military engagement and presence and the aggressive language of e.g. the defense minister is also a demonstration of the will to a lion-like domination. The opposite are the sentiments of inferiors. "They are sentiments of subordination, affection, reverence, fear. They are indispensable to the constitution of animal societies ... [and] to the ordering of human societies" (1963, p. 687, §1156). In the aftermath of September 11 the common man in the US was eager to experience strong leadership and he accepted to give power to the government (US Patriot Act) which would seem impossible without the attacks. The "sentiment of authority may to a greater or lesser extent become disengaged from the person and attached to the symbol, real or presumed, of authority. Hence the importance for those in authority of "keeping up appearances" – "prestige," the outward semblance of superiority" (1963, p. 688, §1157). Finally, we have the need of group approbation (sub-genus $\varepsilon 3$). "The need that the individual feels for being well regarded by his group, for winning its approval, is a very powerful sentiment. On it human society may be said to rest. But it works in silence" (1963, p. 690, §1160).

We will only mention shortly the sex residue. Pareto is not interested in mere sexual appetite, he focuses on it "only in so far as it influences theories, modes of thinking – as a residue" (1963, p. 807, §1324).The last main category is class V: individual integrity of the individual and his appurtenances and possessions. "To defend one's own things and strive to increase their quantity are two operations that frequently merge. So defence of integrity and development of personality are two operations that may differ little or even be one and the same" (1963, p. 727, §1207).

What Pareto seems to have in mind here is "interest." But an example in his first sub-category, sentiments of resistance to alterations in the social equilibrium, shows the non-logical aspect: in ancient Greece, a citizen who does not own slaves fells the wrong that is done to the slave-owner in taking the slave away and making all Greeks free men. It disturbs the prevailing equilibrium on which also depend the interests of the non-slave owners in a general way. Another example is the rather infrequent occurrence of murder. "The sentiment of direct self-preservation has but slight influence in this case. But another sentiment comes into play and functions vigorously: a sentiment of revulsion against anything disturbing to the social equilibrium as it has existed and is accepted by the individual" (1963, p. 729, §1213). The support of the death penalty in the US may to a high degree be explained by this sentiment (we skip the sentiments of equality in inferiors). Pareto's next main category is the restoration of integrity by acts pertaining to the individuals whose integrity has been impaired. "The sense of integrity is among the most powerful sentiments human beings have ... What is known as "remorse" is a manifestation of the concept of altered integrity. The person who violates a certain norm that it has been his habit to observe feels ill at ease from that very fact. He is conscious of being somehow less than he was before. To escape from that painful state of mind, he looks about for some means of removing the strain, of restoring his former integrity" (1963, p. 743, §§1240-1241).

This strain can also be oriented towards imaginary or abstract subjects. "The persistence of an abstraction (II-δ) endows it with a personality, the integrity of which may be impaired; and any person with a deep feeling for the abstraction also feels the offence to its integrity, not only as a thing belonging to himself, but also as something belonging to his group" (1963, p. 786, §1296). The interesting next subdivision is the restoration of integrity by acts pertaining to the offender (we skip imaginary or abstract offenders). "The offence frequently affects more or less extensive groups even if it is done to one individual member. Relatives of the victim ... fellow citizens, and even animals – the dog defending its master, for example – may feel the offence as done to them, that their integrity has been altered; and so the need of a restoration of integrity may arise in them and prompt them to react against the offender. Whence, in their many varieties, the obligation of vengeance and the right to blood-money ... The integrity of the citizens of the civilized country is restored at the expense of the inhabitants of the uncivilized country [after bombarding, Pareto's example]. The sum of sentiments designated by the term "hatred" may be at least partially classed with this variety. Fear very often lies at the bottom of hatred both in men and in animals" (1963, pp. 798-799, §1313). We cannot follow Pareto's lucid analysis but it seems evident that the merciless bombarding of Afghanistan while tens of thousands of Afghani were dying for hunger may find an explanation in this residue.

5. CONCLUSION

With this short recapitulation of Pareto's theory of residues we wanted to present their basic elements and give examples in how far they may help explain non-logical actions which cannot be explained by sophisticated information cost arguments. It may be repeated that Pareto argues in an evolutionary, Darwinian way. Behind the residues are sentiments and drives which were more or less functional in the development of the human species and which have strong corollaries in animal behavior. From a logical point of view, many of these residues are non-functional today but they help understand many occurrences in the real world which are beyond the capabilities of rational man or rational choice explanations.

Pareto focused exclusively on the non-logical part of human action in his sociology and does not apply his economic theory beyond economic subjects in the narrow sense. In so far public choice is a genuine complement. Pareto develops what may be called an irrational choice theory. He shares many theoretical points of view with Schumpeter. Schumpeter presents a very abstract alternative theory of political economy in which irrational factors play an important role. Pareto's theory of residues may function at least as a microfoundation of his political economy. It should be borne in mind that the theory of residues was a tentative proposal with respect to the full set of relevant residues. Further investigations may change, enlarge or reduce Pareto's classification.

APPENDIX

Pareto's residue classes (1963, pp. 516-519, §888)

CLASS I

INSTINCT FOR COMBINATIONS (§§889-990)

I-α. Generic combinations (§§892-909)
I-β. Combinations of similars or opposites (§§910-43)
- I-β1. Generic likeness or oppositeness (§§913-21)
- I-β2. Unusual things and exceptional occurrences (§§922-28)
- I-β3. Objects and occurrences inspiring awe or terror (§§929-31)
- I-β4. Felicitous state associated with good things; infelicitious state, with bad (§§932-36)
- I-β5. Assimilation: physical consumption of substances to get effects of associable, and more rarely of opposite, character (§§937-43)

I-γ. Mysterious workings of certain things; mysterious effects of certain acts (§§944-65)
- I-γ1. Mysterious operations in general (§§947-57)
- I-γ2. Mysterious linkings of names and things (§§958-65)

I-δ. Need for combining residues (§§966-71)
I-ε. Need for logical developments (§§972-75)
I-ζ. Faith in the efficacy of combinations (§§976-90)

CLASS II

GROUP-PERSISTENCES (PERSISTENCE OF AGGREGATES) (§§991-1088)

II-α. Persistence of relations between a person and other persons and places (§§1015-51)

- II-α1. Relationships of family and kindred groups (§§1016-40)
- II-α2. Relations with places (§§1041-42)
- II-α3. Relationships of social class (§§1043-51)

II-β. Persistence of relations between the living and the dead (§§1052-55)
II-γ. Persistence of relations between a dead person and the things that belonged to him in life (§§1056-64)
II-δ. Persistence of abstractions (§§1065-67)
II-ε. Persistence of uniformities (§1068)
II-ζ. Sentiments transformed into objective realities (§1069)
II-η. Personifications (§§1070-85)
II-θ. Need of new abstractions (§§1086-88)

CLASS III

NEED OF EXPRESSING SENTIMENTS BY EXTERNAL ACTS (ACTIVITY, SELF-EXPRESSION) (§§1089-1112)

III-α. Need of "doing something" expressing itself in combinations (§§1092-93)
III-β. Religious ecstasies (§§1094-1112)

CLASS IV

RESIDUES CONNECTED WITH SOCIALITY (§§1113-1206)

IV-α. Particular societies (§1114)
IV-β. Need of uniformity (§§1115-32)

- IV-β1. Voluntary conformity on the part of the individual (§§1117-25)
- IV-β2. Uniformity enforced upon others (§§1126-29)
- IV-β3. Neophobia (§§1130-32)

IV-γ. Pity and cruelty (§§1133-44)

- IV-γ1. Self-pity extended to others (§§1138-41)
- IV-γ2. Instinctive repugnance to suffering (§§1142-43)
- IV-γ3. Reasoned repugnance to useless sufferings (§1144)

IV-δ. Self-sacrifice for the good of others (§§1145-52)

- IV-δ1. Risking one's life (§1148)
- IV-δ2. Sharing one's property with others (§§1149-52)

IV-ε. Sentiments of social ranking; hierarchy (§§1153-62)

- IV-ε1. Sentiments of superiors (§1155)
- IV-ε2. Sentiments of inferiors (§§1156-59)
- IV-ε3. Need of group approbation (§§1160-62)

IV-ζ. Asceticism (§§1163-1206)

CLASS V

INTEGRITY OF THE INDIVIDUAL AND HIS APPURTENANCES (§§1207-1323)

V-α. Sentiments of resistance to alterations in the social equilibrium (§§1208-19)
V-β. Sentiments of equality in inferiors (§§1220-28)

V-γ. Restoration of integrity by acts pertaining to the individual whose integrity has been impaired (§§1229-1311)
  V-γ1. Real subjects (§§1240-95)
  V-γ2. Imaginary or abstract subjects (§§1296-1311)
V-δ. Restoration of integrity by acts pertaining to the offender (vengeance, "getting even") (§1312)
  IV-δ1. Real offender (§§1313-19)
  IV-δ2. Imaginary or abstract offender (§§1320-23)

CLASS VI

THE SEX RESIDUE (§§1324-96)

NOTES

1. See the overviews in Perrin (1967), Tommissen (1968), Bilous and Quirk (1970), Wood and McLure (eds.) (1999), Blaug (ed.) (1992). For an appealing introduction see Pietri-Tonelli et al. (1994), for the sociological debate see e.g. Peukert (1992).
2. We will not discuss Pareto's assumption of the prevalence of logical action in the economy. As we will see below, behavioral finance teaches us, that this is not necessarily so (Shiller 2000).

REFERENCES

Backhaus, J. (1999). "Pareto on public choice". *Vilfredo Pareto*, Vol. 4, ed. J.C. Wood and M. McLure. London, 395-407.
Bilous, J. and Quirk, J.H. (1970). "Interest in Pareto's sociology: An essay in the quantitative history of social science". *Cahiers Vilfredo Pareto*, 20, 145-164.
Blaug, M. (ed.). (1992). *Vilfredo Pareto (1848-1923)*. Aldershot.
Downs, A. (1957). *An Economic Theory of Democracy*. New York.
Goldberg, J. and Nitzsch, R. (2000), *Behavioral Finance*. 2nd ed. Munich.
Kuttner, R. (1998), *Everything for Sale*. New York.
Macpherson, C.B. (1999). "Pareto's *General Sociology:* The problem of method in the social sciences". *Vilfredo Pareto*, Vol. 1, ed. J.C. Wood and M. McLure. London, 286-297.
Mitchell, W.C. (1984). "Schumpeter and public choice. Part I: Precursor of public choice?". *Public Choice*, 42, 73-88.
Pareto, V. (1963). *The Mind and Society: A Treatise on General Sociology*. 2 vols. New York.
Perrin, G. (1967). "Bibliographie relative à la sociologie de Pareto". *Cahiers Vilfredo Pareto*, 11, 87-102.
Peukert, H. (2002). "The missing seventh chapter in Schumpeter's Theory of Economic Development". *Schumpeter: Social Scientist*, hg. J. Backhaus, forthcoming.
Peukert, H. (1998). *Das Handlungsparadigma in der Nationalökonomie*. Marburg.
Peukert, H. (1992). *Parsons/Pareto/Habermas*. Idstein.
Pietri-Tonelli, A. et al. (1994). *Vilfredo Pareto*. Houndmills.
Prisching, M. (1995). "The limited rationality of democracy: Schumpeter as the founder of irrational choice theory". *Critical Review*, 9, 301-324.
Samuels, W.J. (1974). *Pareto on Politics*. North-Holland.

Schumpeter, J.A. (1996). *Capitalism, Socialism and Democracy*. Introduction by R. Swedberg. 5th ed. London.

Schumpeter, J.A. (1912). *Theorie der wirtschaftlichen Entwicklung*. Leipzig.

Schumpeter, J.A. (1952). *The Theory of Economic Development*. Cambridge.

Shiller, R.J. (2000). *Irrational Exuberance*. Princeton.

Tommissen, P. (1968). "A propos d'une bibliographie de M. Guy Perrin sur la sociologie de Pareto". *Cahiers Vilfredo Pareto*, 15, 231-237.

Tullock, G. (1998). "Public choice". *The New Palgrave*, Vol. 3, ed. Eatwell, J. et al. Macmillan, 1040-1044.

Udehn, L. (1996). *The Limits of Public Choice*. London.

Wohlgemuth, M. (2001). *Schumpeterian Political Economy vs. Downsian Public Choice*. Mimeo.

Wood, J.C. and McLure, M. (eds.) (1999). *Vilfredo Pareto: Critical Assessments*. 4 vols. London.

8. Economic Equilibria and the Balancing Act between Total and Partial Analysis

Roland Dillmann† and Hans Frambach

University of Wuppertal, Germany

Abstract

Equilibria have long been central to economic thought and theory. Extensive areas of theoretical economics culminate in the idea of equilibrium and in the question of what quantities determine equilibrium. Even in the analysis of disequilibria the idea of equilibria often serves as a standard of comparison. Walras, the Nestor of economic equilibrium analysis, and regarded as the founder of total analysis, tried to present a simultaneous equilibrium on different markets. However, with reference to Walras' "mechanistic" point of view, equilibria are often interpreted as a quasi-natural state, but this ignores Walras' understanding of equilibrium as an ideal state, which for example helps to explain the adjustment process within disequilibria. While partial analysis only investigates the principle reason, in his concept of general equilibrium Walras emphasized the separability of influences and their intercorrelation, the concept of total analysis was recognized as an appropriate method of representation. But even the use of total analysis, especially when expressed in mathematical terms, imposes limits. Assuming non-linear functions (e.g., utility functions) the economist has the problem of empirical foundation. Using linear functions, which is exactly what Walras did in most cases, actually implies the "whole as the sum of all single causes." We are convinced that Walras intended to explain dependencies of economic quantities on the basis of a non-linear context. But verbal explanation and its transformation into mathematics are two different things. Nevertheless, even nowadays we use linear models because the mathematical representation of interaction fails for lack of more detailed knowledge of the quantitative context (making simplicity a matter of principle in case of doubt). It is Walras' ideas on representation of complex structures and *not* the attempt to transform them into mathematical terms which will be emphasized as his outstanding achievement – his ideas were of a more far-reaching content than his mathematics. It will also be argued that Walras' ideas can be taken as an excellent introduction into a well-founded structuring of microeconomic problems, they also allow us to gain an insight into fundamental economic ideas such as utility, exchange and equilibrium, and they enlighten on the general discussion of mutual dependency of economic quantities. A deep knowledge of the interaction of economic variables is an indispensable tool for reconciling scarce means and ends or, more generally speaking, for rational behaviour itself. We are trying to give Walras economic profundity and breadth in an area where it is "normally" denied him by critics of equilibrium theory. Equilibria, linearities and non-linearities, total vs. partial analysis are the keywords of our paper.

Keywords: Cournot, Economic Analysis, Economic Equilibria, Marshall, Pareto, Partial Analysis, Production Function, Total Analysis, Walras

JEL classification: B13, D50

1. EQUILIBRIUM AND ECONOMIC ANALYSIS – SOME GENERAL POSITIONS

In the history of economic thought *the Cantillon-Quesnay-Tableau* is known as a first method giving an idea of the interdependency of economic quantities including its "balancing" forces (conditions of equilibrium). The *Tableau* delivers a graphic picture of general interdependence by means of drastic simplification of the economic system into three interacting sectors (farmers, landowners, artisans). Accordingly, the *selective* examination of a simplified economic structure can, to a certain extent, in itself be seen as a method of *partial analysis*. In contrast to the analysis of the effects single independent variables have on a dependent quantity, the study of economic states as circular flows and therefore the integration of the interdependence of many variables, as presented in the *Tableau*, represent a more general, "total" view. This total view seems to be preferable to the partial point of view.

1.1. Partial Analysis and Total Analysis in Literature: Cournot, Pareto, Walras, Marshall

But even if we succeed in explaining all the variables to be considered, including their interdependencies (*total analysis*) within an economic model, the application of the discoveries should be a better approximation to our view of reality and should not be confused with reality itself. Obviously even total analysis is a special kind of model, an abstraction of the real world. In this respect total analysis can be regarded as a *partial analysis of reality*. Thus, an important question is, how "total" a total analysis can be?

A well known example of partial analysis in economic literature is the demand curve invented by Augustin Cournot and Alfred Marshall representing the demand for a good a purchaser wants to buy at a certain price solely as a mathematical function of the price of the product. Cournot (1963, pp. 38-45) assumed a function $f(p)$ expressing the law of demand or of the market. He formalizes his view of demand by introducing a continuous function where the variations have opposite signs ("an increase in price will correspond with a diminution of the demand"; p. 41). Marshall represented the demand curve as a function $p = f(x)$. At a price p the consumer is willing to buy x units of a product – all the other possible effects other factors than the price could have on the decision to buy the good, including, for example, the influence of marginal utility of money, are totally neglected (Marshall, 1922, pp. 334-6, Mathem. App., II, VI, pp. 838-42). In "Principles of Economics" Marshall (1922, p. 99) defined the general law of demand on the basis of the principle of diminishing utility: "The greater the amount to be sold, the smaller must be the price at which it is offered in order that it may find purchasers; or, in other words, the amount demanded increases with a fall in price, and diminishes with a rise in price".

As another example for partial analysis, in Book V of "Principles" (Theory of the Equilibrium of Demand and Supply) Marshall generally discusses instruments of economic analysis under a ceteris paribus condition, and the way economic units of different size, such as small or big firms, operate (Marshall, 1922, e.g., pp. 361-74, 459). Also the term "partial analysis" very often represents the analysis of a single market or a small group under the condition of one dominant influence (regarded by Marshall as a "normal" situation). If conditions change, the result of partial analysis will also change more or less. But how far can results of a (partial) analysis drawn under certain conditions be generalised and what is the meaning of such results for the system as a whole? The advantage is evident: The more an issue is narrowed, the more simply (others would say exactly) can it be handled and the more it helps towards treating broader issues in which that narrow issue is contained, but – even as Marshall (1922, p. 366) himself has already seen – "the less closely does it correspond to real life". The description "general law of demand" should be noted because of the obvious partial analytic character of its derivation.

Partial analysis in an empirical sense is justified when the (partial) industrial branches, firms or other special economic units are so small that changes in their variables have *no* influence on the other parts of the system, i.e. the whole system. In this case the effects of economic variables on the outside world (the other sectors) are only marginal and can be neglected. But we need to be careful, as Schumpeter (1954 p. 991) has pointed out, when results of partial analysis, which have proved correct for small sectors, are transferred to the economy as a whole: here the results can turn out to be complete nonsense.

Another advantage of partial analysis is the possibility to approach the phenomena to be explained in a quick and easy way. But such an approximation implies neglect of the effects of those variables which are not considered in the model but which, nonetheless, are important in the real economy. The restrictions the partial analysis is accompanied by were already recognized by authors such as Léon Walras and Vilfredo Pareto. Even Cournot, whose observations about the Law of Demand and the theory of Monopoly, for example, were of provisional character for Marshall, realized that "in reality the economic system is a whole of which all the parts are connected and react to each other" (Cournot, 1963, p. 108). He concluded, that for a complete and rigorous solution of a problem which only concerns some parts of the economic system, it is necessary to take the entire system into consideration. But such a project "would surpass the powers of mathematical analysis and of our practical methods of calculation, even if the values of all the constants could be assigned to them numerically" (p. 108). This demonstrates Cournot's conviction about the limits of mathematical analysis and economic methods. Therefore Cournot justified the treatment of economic problems by partial analysis, understood as a "certain kind of approximation" which uses mathematical analysis (p. 108).

Walras not only criticized Cournot's partial analysis, he also criticized that of v. Mangoldt, Marshall, and especially Auspitz/v. Liebens. In the article "Observations on the Auspitz and Lieben principle of the theory of prices"[1] Walras asserted that demand and supply curves of products which were solely derived from the prices of these products could never be exact. A change of only one product price would always cause a disturbance of the whole equilibrium situation which requires an adjustment of all the elements involved (Walras, 1977, pp. 484-6). This is obviously a different view of the problem which was already raised by Cournot.

> The *demand* curve ..., i.e. the curve representing the *quantity sold* as a function of the *selling price*, cannot be regarded as a rigorously exact curve. The quantity sold of any product is a function not only of its own selling price, but also of the selling prices of all other products and the prices of all productive services. Messrs. Auspitz and Lieben assume that the selling prices of other products and the prices of all productive services can be held constant, while the selling prices of the productive under consideration varies. Theoretically, they have no right to do this. The selling prices of products and the prices of productive services are mutually interrelated. Whenever the price of a given product is changed, the prices of the productive services and consequently the selling prices of the other commodities are also changed. Strange as it may seem, these very authors, Messrs. Auspitz and Lieben, have quite wrongly taken me to task, in their preface, for a fault which I have good reason here to lay at their door, namely, that of treating demands which are functions of several variables as functions of a single variable. (Walras, 1977, pp. 484-6)

Pareto followed the principle, "that if we want to be completely rigorous, every theory is false in the sense that it does not agree with and can never agree with reality" (Pareto, 1971, p. 116, see also p. 337). The researcher only knows ideal phenomena, which more or less approximate the concrete phenomena. The theory which comes closest to a description of the phenomena will be chosen as an approach to explanation. The manner of approaching reality using theories which are increasingly in accord with it, and – as Pareto states – which in consequence generally become more and more complex, is what he calls the *method of successive approximations* (Pareto, 1971, pp. 8-9). This is a very modern methodological view.

To treat a problem in theory it is necessary to eliminate all facts regarded as inessential. But, in contrast to Cournot, Pareto preferred total analysis as a realizable and more suitable problem-solving method. Pareto assesses theories which explain that problems looked at from a very partial point of view (for example, theories which connect only values or prices and final degree of utility) are not very useful in political economy (Pareto, 1971, p. 180). Consequently, Pareto's view fits into general positions of modern microeconomics; for example, Kelvin Lancaster: "Partial analysis becomes less and less appropriate the more the effect changes in the particular market have on the economy as a whole. It is ultimately a matter of *fact*, not of hypothesis, whether partial analysis is appropriate in any given case" (Lancaster, 1974, p. 278). But it also follows that partial and total analysis are hardly compatible. In the state of general equilibrium the prices and quantities of all products are determined simultaneously, whereas in partial analysis single prices and quantities (for every product) are determined one after the other. This means that total analysis can never be equal to the sum of all the single (partial) effects, and therefore partial analysis becomes useless for interpreting total processes. Coming back to Pareto, it seems that Pareto believed more in the capability of mathematics than Cournot did because Pareto considered mathematics (in contrast to ordinary logic) as being capable of "studying the relation of cause and effect" even when it is "a matter of relations of mutual dependence" (Pareto, 1971, p. 180). With this "broader" understanding of pure economics one can say that Pareto evidently regards partial analysis only as a first approximation but he clearly prefers total analysis in the sense of viewing the effects of all variables considered. Consequently, Walras and Pareto saw equilibrium theory as a method to record the whole range of causes whereas partial analysis primarily searches for the main cause.

1.2. Partial Analysis and Total Analysis: A Model-Dependent View

Let us now discuss more intensively the consequences of the necessity of simplification in theory to show first that judgement about the character of an analysis has to be relativised on the underlying model and second that there are strong connections between total and partial analysis in empirical work (see Figure 1).

In theory we differ between endogeneous and exogeneous variables of a model; it is useful to introduce a further term to meet the consequences of the necessity of simplification in our description of the relation between total and partial analysis. One method of simplification is to regard economic quantities as constant in a model whereas they are judged as variable in reality. As

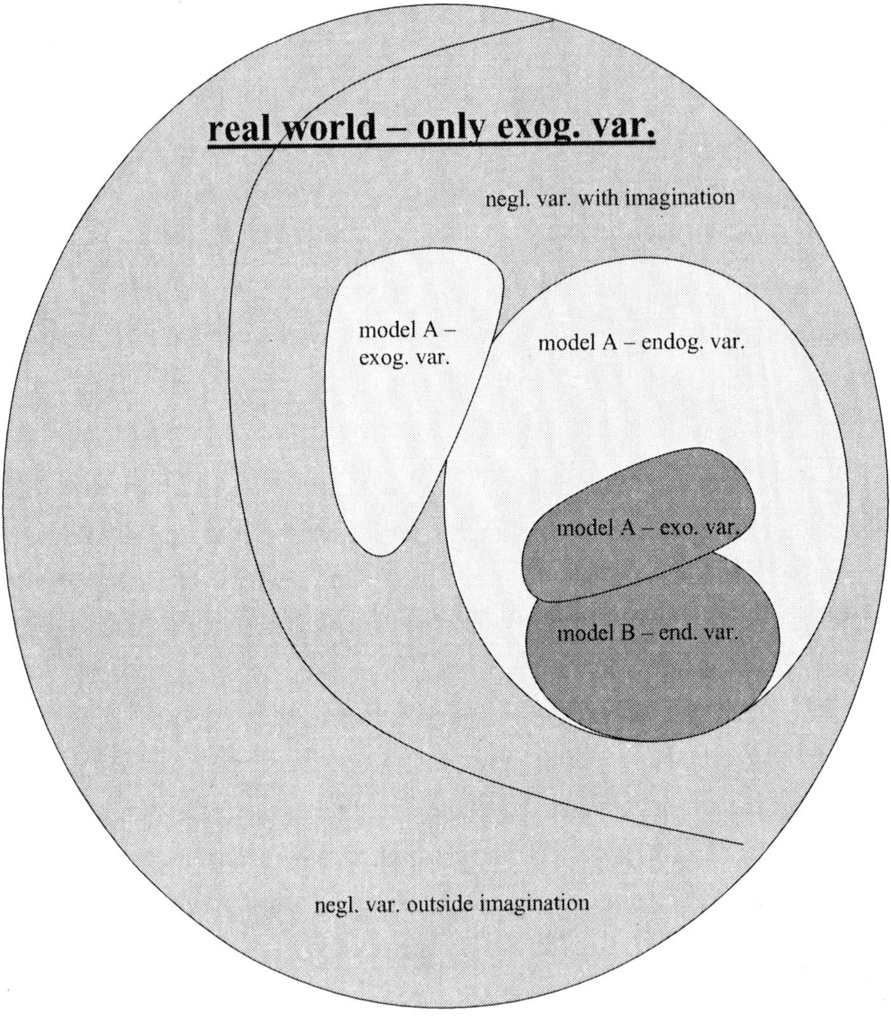

Figure 1.

long as the researcher believes that the simplified picture of reality is sophisticated enough to make a fruitful analysis possible, this procedure is necessary to clarify the derivation of his statements. The decision as to which variable quantities in reality should be treated as constant in theory is a very important task of the model builder, but the decision has to be regarded as subjective. Let us introduce the term "neglected variables by a model" to treat some variable economic quantities as constant in the context of a special model. It may happen that another researcher includes some of the neglected variables in his model, but accepts the rest of the original model. Consequently, he proposes a model A, which he regards as a generalisation of model B. The criterion for generalisation is the following: handling the variables neclected in B but not in A as constants, one gets during the analysis of model A all the consequences of model B. In this case new theorems, relativizing the consequences of model B, may be derived in model A on the basis of the variability of some quantities regarded as constant in model B but introduced as variables in model A.

Then we can define the terms of partial and total analysis more closely: we speak of partial analysis in terms of model B when model B contains exogeneous and endogeneous variables, we speak of a total analysis in terms of model B if all variables are interpreted as endogeneous; from the viewpoint of model A the analysis of model B has to be regarded as partial analysis because model B is a specialisation of model A and the variables additionally introduced in model A have to be interpreted as constants with respect to model B.

One further aspect is of importance: we only speak about total analysis when a model covers several markets, that means if the model has a certain minimal complexity.

1.3. Partial Analysis and Total Analysis: An Empirical View

A well known instrument to regard partial analysis as a first draft of a total analysis is given by Taylor's theorem which develops a function by its value and the values of the first n derivatives at a special point. Using Taylor's theorem it can easily be shown that the total view does not reach further than the partial view in the case of functions of the form

$$f(x_1, \ldots, x_n) = \sum_{i=1}^{n} a_i x_i + b \text{ (affine-linear functions, linear, if } b = 0)$$

because then the total effect can be demonstrated as being equal to the sum of the partial effects. That means that total analysis is only more informative than partial analysis if important non-linearities exist which make possible a description of interdependencies between the variables. Non-linearities which lead to an approach of separable functions only are not enough to make total analysis more informative than partial analysis, because the interdependencies between the variables are the reason why the complete reaction is different from the sum of the individual reactions.

In empirical work we are confronted with a problem of epistemology: on which information basis should a non-linear function be selected? Normally, the information needed to fill the gap between our qualitative "knowledge" (better "pre-judgments") and the information necessary to give our pre-judgments a mathematical description by the adequate choice of functional dependencies, is not available, and the choice of the functions is made solely on the basis of the methodological principle of simplicity; this argument, and not the economist's belief in the linearity of the world, is the reason for the broad use of linear functions in economics, especially in econometrics. This argument shows the narrow limits of the advantages of a total analysis in empirical research resulting from the problem of epistemology underlying the choice of the functions.

2. WALRAS AND EQUILIBRIUM – SOME INTERPRETATIONS

From the methodological point of view Walras' mathematical approach of price determination represents the first step towards modern general equilibrium analysis. In the following section we shortly go into Walras' equilibrium approach and ask how far he has met his own demand, to what extent he influenced later research programmes (especially the proofs of the existence of a general equilibrium solution on the basis of "fixed-point theory"), and what his ideas about the most fundamental notion, economic equilibrium, were. Because we believe that Walras interpreted the state of equilibrium rather as an analytical kind of reference than an economic fact, persuing a "broad" ("total") kind of analysis, methodological importance is attached to his work in the sense of an interplay of partial and total analysis.

Equilibria have always been central to economic thought and theory. Even the discussion of disequilibria requires the idea of equilibrium. The name Walras stands for the foundation of a non-linear theory of general equilibrium. *More exactly, the underlying functions as the mathematical tool to describe causal dependencies may be regarded as non-linear, but they are not specified to a degree that they can be used in an empirical investigation.* Following Walras (1977, p. 35) his theory "contains a mathematical solution of the problem of the determination of current prices and also a scientific formulation of the law of supply and demand (...)".

2.1. The Model

He presents his analysis in four steps. The first step serves to explain exchange in a world of two goods, the second step generalizes an exchange theory to a world of n goods. There is no further economic change when the subjective rate of exchange of two goods for every acteur is equal to the quotient of their prices, every demand finds its supply and vice versa. If an acteur tries to increase the quantity of a good by exchange, we speak of individual demand, in the other case of individual supply. An acteur demands or supplies a good, he does not do both. Supply and demand are derived from some utility curves and a principle of utility maximization which says in particular that the subjective exchange rate has to be equal to the "objective" exchange rate (defined by the quotient of prices). The transformation of his utility approach into a function to describe the demand for a good dependent on all good prices is highly non-linear.[2]

The sum of the values of all individual supplies and demands has to be zero, therefore we get only $n-1$ independent individual demand and supply functions (Walras' Law). By aggregation we get $n-1$ independent curves. Aggregating the individual functions, if we sum up all individual demand, we get the aggregated demand function, in the same manner we get the aggregated supply function. Further n equations are given by the fact that an exchange in equilibrium is only possible if aggregated supply and demand are equal for all n goods.

In a third step the basis for exchange is extended by the introduction of land services, labor services, capital services. In addition to the goods, the acteurs can exchange the different services. The production sphere is introduced as the place where the different services can be transformed into goods by an adequate combination of these services. Different combinations are possible (substitutive production function). He considers the situation where utilized capital services are reproduced and the capital stock remains unchanged.

In a world with a substitutive production function no change of the plans is necessary if the marginal productivity of every resource equals the disadvantage of its loss, if the supply of every productive service equals the demand of the productive service and if the demand for the produced goods equals the supply of the produced goods. Every acteur is regarded as being an entrepreneur who supplies his labour, land and resources as services. It is assumed that the natural price of a good is given by the production costs of these three services. This allows us to determine the price of all produced goods on the basis of the costs of the different services.

Although using substitutive production functions and choosing the minimal cost solution, Walras first assumes an economy without new capital goods (stationary economy) and he argues with fixed quotients between produced goods and the productive inputs.

Later he introduces new capital goods, and in spite of a change of scarcity between capital and the other productive factors, during his analysis he keeps the assumption of fixed capital coefficients. This may be the reason for the interpretation that Walras' analysis was a linear one. The equilibrium describes a situation where the consumers and producers on every market, pursuing their own interests under certain restrictions, simultaneously reach an equilibrium among all the considered markets. In this state all demand and all supply is satisfied.

In a fourth step Walras generalizes the assumption of a stationary economy, he includes the increase of capital goods, money and the rate of interest. He assures us, that the cost price of every new capital good is equal to the discounted net return of the last unit of the new capital (two equations for every capital good, one for the cost price and the other for the discounted return), that complete output equals consumption + investment, finally money is the new numéraire, so that we have for every good a price relation to the numéraire. In spite of the change of the capital stock because of saving and investment decisions, in Chapter V Walras does not discuss the consequences on the variation of production coefficients; they remain constant.

2.2. Walras' Equilibrium Analysis

Equilibrium in production, like equilibrium in exchange, is an ideal and not a real state. It never happens in the real world that the selling price of any given product is absolutely equal to the cost of productive services that enter that product, or that the effective demand and supply of services or products are absolutely equal. Yet equilibrium is a normal state, in the sense that it is the state towards which things spontaneously tend under a régime of free competition in exchange and production (Walras, 1977, p. 224).

From Walras' point of view in the real world we observe disequilibria, but if we try to define disequilibrium analytically, this cannot be done without the concept of equilibrium. Recognizing the impossibility of implementing current economic plans completely, acteurs try to overcome the actual disequilibrium by adjustment processes whose orientation has to be based on an idea of economic equilibrium, i.e. a state where all economic plans are co-ordinated and nobody sees the necessity to change his plans. Walras' interpretation of the meaning of the concept of equilibrium in economics may be far more indirect than is often attributed to him when he is regarded as an economist for whom equilibrium is a natural state of the real world, a position which Walras himself has critically ascribed to Say.

Let us exemplify Walras' equilibrium analysis taking the production sector into consideration. The analysis in the other sectors seems to be very similar. Its core is a special co-ordination (groping) process.

For the analysis of equilibrium Walras proposed a co-ordination process based on the assumption that every producer chooses on his market the quantity which is determined by the cost price of his good, keeping the other prices constant. This leads to equilibrium when all other prices are unchanged. The interdependence between all acteurs is to be seen by the new price vector necessary to bring together demand and supply. But this new price vector is not equal to the cost vector, determined by the quantities offered. We have described one step of the underlying adjustment process which is stable if the influence of the other prices is marginal on the market and the changed price is the dominant one. This assumption lies behind Walras' analysis:

> This adjustment is what might be called a consequence of the first order, which is of prime importance so far as the price of (B) [the quantity offered; D/F] is concerned. The same adjustment might even restore equilibrium (in the market as a whole), if the total amount $d_b p_b$ spent by each and every party on the consumption of (B) remains unchanged. But since each individual's outlay on (B) would undoubtedly change in every case, increasing for some parties while decreasing for others, whether the quantity of (B) manufactured expanded or contracted, it follows that those parties whose outlay on (B) increased would have to sell a quantity of various (other) commodities, which would tend to depress (their) prices, while those parties whose outlay on (B) decreased would have to buy a quantity of various (other) commodities, which would tend to raise (their) prices. This would be a consequence of the second order, which, so far as the prices of (B), (C), (D) ... are concerned, turns out to be of a minor importance (...). (Walras, 1977, p. 246)

This is an assumption that can be mathematically formulated in a sense that fixed-point theorems can be utilized on the basis of contraction arguments. For such assumptions see Hicks (1968, Chaper II: General Equilibrium); they are repeated in Henderson-Quandt (1971); another assumption is based on a theorem of Sperner and operates on the normalization that the sum of all prices (including the numéraire) is 1 (see, for example, Border, 1986).

Let us show more extensively the way from equilibrium analysis to the concept of fixed points. We start with a given initial set of goods and services of all acteurs. Acteurs try to increase their welfare by exchanging parts of their set for parts of the sets belonging to the others. On the basis of given prices for services we observe an over-demand and over-supply of some services and goods. This vector of over-supply and over-demand causes an adjustment of prices. This can be formalized by the definition of a function of price-space in price-space. This function assigns to every point in the price space the new price resulting from the adjustment process as a reaction of over-supply or over-demand. In a situation where demand and supply are equal, no price adjustment is necessary, we assign the price itself to the price behind the equilibrium of supply and demand. We introduce the concept "fixed point of the function for a point which is assigned to itself by a function". We have reformulated the question of existence and determination of equilibrium as a question of existence and determination of fixed points of a function and have made available a wide reaching mathematical theory for dealing with our economic problem.

The mathematical theory of fixed points offers solution possibilities with the help of different principles. Fixed point theorems are proved on the basis of assumptions making possible the use of the contraction principle. The groping process introduced by Walras may be interpreted in terms of the contraction principle. Other ways to prove fixed point theorems start with functions of compact spaces in themselves. They are utilized in economic theory by normalizing the price vector in a form that the sum of all prices (including the price of the numéraire) equals 1. For an elementary overview of the mathematical fixed-point theory, see Istratescu (1981). A bridge to the current economic discussion is provided by Border (1986).

In earlier treatises Walras counted only variables and equations, possibly a further reason for the interpretation of the linearity of his model.

We said that Walras kept the production coefficients constant during his analysis in Chapter V in spite of changes of the capital stock. This constancy of the production coefficients is debated in Chapter VII where Walras explicitly introduces the difference between economic progress and technical progress. Economic progress means the change to other points along the isoquants of the production function because of a change of the raretés. Technical progress will change the production function, and as a consequence the isoquants. Walras explicitly reduces his work to an analysis of economic progress and does not propose a time dependent change of the production function. Insofar his analysis stays static, a problem not yet solved. Instead he discusses the change in prices because of a change in the rareté of land services. He does this by assuming a stable production function. But here he develops what we call today the minimal cost combination as the optimal point of production.

2.3. The Problem of the Variability of Production Functions

With regard to the question as to what is to be seen as constant and what as variable during analysis Walras remarks: "The theorist has the right to assume that the underlying price determinants are invariant over the period he has chosen to use in its formulation of the law of equilibrium prices. But, once this formulation has been completed, it is his duty to remember that the forces that underlie prices are by their nature variable, and consequently he must formulate the law of the variation of equilibrium prices" (Walras, 1977, p. 146). We can follow this argument, but in the production sphere it is interesting that Walras decided not to give a formulation of technical progress and only to investigate economic progress. That can only mean that the analysis of economic progress was regarded as the economically important task, and consequently we can argue that free competition was emphasized by Walras because of its allocation qualities.

Therefore an important part of Walras' work, estimated by him as pure theoretics, but as an important basis for the art (art in the sense of applied economics), has actually lost importance: since Schumpeter's position that competition is the relevant force in the production of new products and new productive possibilities (to be described by the change of the production function over time, especially by an economic theory of technical progress) and that co-ordination by free competition is only a mechanism of optimal allocation of the resources, the model of free competition has lost its function as an ideal for competition policies because the dynamic aspects of the co-ordination mechanism are neglected. Walras' justification of free competition as the ideal co-ordination mechanism for society has historical rather than practical importance today because wide parts of the competition discussion followed Schumpeter's judgment about the importance of the dynamic function of competition.

3. CONCLUSION

What can we learn from Walras today? First he formulated extensive areas of modern microeconomics at a time when fixed-point theorems were not available. But the practical relevance of this part of modern microeconomics is dubious, and here we have the point where time has overtaken the scientific work of Walras: the basis for emphazising free competition as an adequate ideal for competition policies. His work has lost the ability to be regarded as the foundation of economic science for economics, understood as an art.

His importance to modern-day economists has to be derived from his methodological views. He formulated a lot of current questions and theoretical concepts (especially the concept of labor services, very close to the modern concept of human capital) and proposed a solution method for the resulting system of equations anticipating the fixed-point discussion, initiated by mathematicians some time later, for example by Banach and Brouwer. He had a very modern idea of the meaning of equilibrium, and his methodological views with respect to the role of mathematics are of current relevance for extensive areas of mainstream economics. His mathematical methods of analysis cannot be called elaborated because the underlying concepts were developed later in mathematics. But he offered an important and fruitful direction and opened it for economics. Being of actual importance, he defended pure science but saw the importance of application and regarded pure theory as fundamental to applications. Here we are at the beginning of his book and his trilogy of science, art and ethics with the categories of truth, usefulness and justice.

NOTES

1. The article was published in 1890 in the *Revue d'économie politique* (reprinted in the Appendix II of Walras "Elements", Ed. Déf.; 1977, pp. 483-8). The cause for Walras' criticism was the first chapter (pp.1-24) and the appropriated appendix (pp. 431-5) of the "Untersuchungen über die Theorie des Preises" (Inquiry into the Theory of Price), a book published by Rudolf Auspitz and Richard Lieben in 1889 (see also, Walras, 1977, p. 483, especially fn. 1).
2. Walras formulates his analysis using cardinally measurable utility, but Pareto showed that measuring utility ordinally allows to realize the same principle because situations of the same utility can be formalized by indifference curves, and indifference curves allow to speak about a subjective exchange rate with respect to the same utility level. Cardinality of the utility measure is not central to the determination of the subjective rate of exchange.

REFERENCES

Auspitz, R. and Lieben, R. (1889). *Untersuchungen über die Theorie des Preises*, Leipzig: Duncker & Humblot.

Blaug, M. (1962). *Economic Theory in Retrospect*, 5th Ed., Orig. Ed. Cambridge: Cambridge University Press.

Border, K.C. (1986). *Fixed Point Theorems with Applications to Economics and Game Theory*, Repr. of the Ed. London, New York, New Rochelle, Melbourne, Sydney: Cambridge University Press.

Cournot, A. (1963). *Researches into the Mathematical Principles of the Theory of Wealth*, Orig. French Ed. 1838, Homewood, IL: Irwin.

Henderson, J.M. and Quandt, R.E. (1971). *Microeconomic Theory, A Mathematical Approach*, 2nd Ed., Orig. Ed. 1958, New York: McGraw-Hill.

Hicks, J.R. (1968). *Value and Capital. An Inquiry into Some Fundamental Principles of Economic Theory*, Repr. of the 2nd Ed. 1946, Orig. Ed. 1939, Oxford: Clarendon Press.

Istratescu, V.I. (1981). *Fixed Point Theory. An Introduction*, Dordrecht, Holland: Reidel Publishing Company.

Lancaster, K. (1974). *Introduction to Modern Microeconomics*, 2nd Ed., Orig. Ed. 1969, Chicago: Rand McNally Publ. Comp.

Marshall, A. (1922). *Principles of Economics. An Introductory Volume*, Repr. of the 8th Ed. 1920, Orig. Ed. 1890, London: Macmillan.

Pareto, V. (1971). *Manual of Political Economy*, transl. of the French edition 1927, New York: A.M. Kelley.

Schumpeter, J.A. (1954). *History of Economic Analysis*, edited by E.B. Schumpeter, New York: Oxford University Press.

Walras, L. (1977). *Elements of Pure Economics or the Theory of Social Wealth*, Repr. of the transl. of the French 4th Ed. (Edition Définitive) 1926, Orig. Ed. 1874, Fairfield: A.M. Kelley.

Walras, L. (1972). *Mathematische Theorie der Preisbestimmung der wirtschaftlichen Güter – Vier Denkschriften*, Repr. of the Orig. Ed. 1881, Glashütten im Taunus: Detlev Auvermann.

9. Two Views on Pareto's Current Relevance*: Warren Samuel's Foreword to *Pareto, Economics and Society*

Michael McLure**

University of Western Australia

Abstract

In the "Foreword" to the book *Pareto, Economics and Society: The Mechanical Analogy*, Warren Samuels observes that, in contrast to his own Paretian research, McLure reformulates and extends Pareto in the 'modern mode.' This presentation considers McLure's Paretian approach to government and policy in light of Samuels' concerns with that approach, especially the reliance on stable and unstable equilibrium analysis and the importance of the methodological distinction between the 'form' and 'substance' of phenomena. It is concluded that, just as 'special' sociology is complemented by Pareto's 'general' sociology, so to is Samuels' *Pareto on Policy* complemented by McLure's approach to Pareto.

Keywords: Pareto, Policy, Path-dependence, Equilibrium, Conformity, Non-conformity

JEL classification: B3

1. INTRODUCTION

In a recently published book, entitled *Pareto, Economics and Society: The Mechanical Analogy* (McLure, 2001), I proposed a particular Paretian approach to the study of government and public policy. The approach was derived from an investigation of the relationship between Pareto's pure economics and general sociology, as suggested by his use of the mechanical analogy in both disciplines.

---

* Conference Proceedings: *The Current Relevance of Léon Walras and Vilfredo Pareto and their Legacy for Modern Political Economy*, Universiteit Maastricht, 14 and 15 June 2001.

** The presenter would like to thank Warren J. Samuels for commenting on a draft of this paper and the anonymous referee for proving several very helpful suggestions. The opinions expressed are those of the presenter, who is also responsible for any errors in the paper.

The "Foreword" that introduces this book was written by Warren J. Samuels (2001), whose work in *Pareto on Policy* (Samuels, 1974) represents a significant point in Paretian research. The main value of the "Foreword" to *Pareto, Economics and Society* (*PES*) derives from the general contrast of my research with Samuels' own approach to Pareto, although it also sheds light on the work being introduced. The contrasts presented are particularly useful points of reference when considering the current relevance of Pareto to the political economy of public policy.

The critical difference between Samuels' approach to Pareto and my own concerns the role of optimisation and equilibrium. Samuels contends that Pareto optimality constitutes an infinitesimally small part of Pareto's total social system (Samuels, 2001, xi), and as a consequence, optimality and equilibrium do not figure prominently in his re-interpretations and extensions of Pareto's social systems. In contrast, optimality and equilibrium are assigned some prominence in *PES*, albeit within Pareto's methodological context where the chance of false determinism from excessive reliance on axiomatic deductions is reduced (by assigning a prominent role to political sociology).

The purpose of this presentation is to discuss Samuels' "Foreword" and the proposed new Paretian approach to politics developed in *PES*, with a view to considering the current relevance of Pareto to the political economy of policy. In doing so, aspects of *PES* that Samuels is "not entirely comfortable with" will be isolated and examined.

Section 2 summarises the main issues that Samuels raises in the "Foreword" to *PES*. Section 3 presents the interpretative frameworks utilised in *PES*, and contrasts this to that adopted in *Pareto on Policy*. Section 4 overviews the main features of the new Paretian framework proposed in *PES* for the study of government and public policy. Samuels' 'discomfort' with this framework is considered in Section 5, as is a tentative suggestion that the two approaches really complement each other. The presentation concludes in Section 6 with comments on the current relevance of Pareto to policy studies and some 'speculation' on his likely future influence on political economy.

2. SAMUELS' "FOREWORD" TO *PES*

Samuels presents Pareto as a great systems theorist whose work embraces theories from a range of social disciplines. While noting a neglect of the larger understanding of his total system, he largely regards this as a consequence of Pareto's decision to emphasise optimality and equilibrium as analytical tools in his economic writing. In regard to the work being introduced, Samuels notes that:

> McLure's work pursues one general line of development, advancing Pareto's mechanistic approach while endeavouring both to maintain something of the

> breadth of his system and to distinguish between conclusions relating to form and to substance. ... The result is not Pareto, it is not as much, if at all, an attempt to restate Pareto in modern terms, as it is a reformulation and extension of Pareto in the modern mode (Samuels, 2001, xii).

Samuels regards the approach taken as legitimate, leading to many insightful conclusions. However, he expresses a 'displeasure' with the modern mode of economics and is 'not entirely comfortable' with what he perceives as a finessing of Pareto's total social system in *PES* to achieve an equilibrium framework (that reduces the openendedness of Pareto's system of interdependence over time). Similarly, he is not comfortable with the application of his own work on Pareto within the interpretative framework used in *PES*.

This discomfort is centred on a perception that much of what is interesting and important in Pareto's work is lost when equilibrium is assigned a prominent role, as it is in the modern mode of economics. This concern is reinforced by Samuels' suggestion that the particular specification of 'positive' theory of public policy in *PES* is narrower than the broadest one found in Pareto (Samuels, 2001, xiii).

3. INTERPRETATIVE FRAMEWORK

Samuels' "Foreword" is mainly directed at the penultimate chapter of the book, which reformulates and extends Pareto's work by outlining a particular Paretian framework for the study of government and public policy. Nevertheless, he also suggests that interpretations of Pareto (as opposed to extensions) are complicated by four factors: the choice of interpretative stand point; the formulation of that stand point; the specification of evolving ideas (which publications are cited); and the basis of comparison (Samuels, 2001, xii).

When the interpretative chapters of *PES* are considered in light of these four factors, it becomes clearer that the result 'is Pareto', at least in the sense that Pareto's methodological approach to science is correctly reflected and his economic and sociological theory is stated in the 'equilibrium' mode. To achieve comparative balance, this is then briefly contrasted to Samuels' approach in *Pareto on Policy*.

3.1. Choice of Interpretative Stand Point

PES presents an interpretation of the relationship between Pareto's pure economic theory and general sociology, and its relevance to the study of political conduct. The primary interpretative standpoint in this work is the 'mechanical analogy'. This was selected because Pareto utilised the mechanical analogy extensively in both economics and sociology over the course of his contribution to science.

In this context, it is essential to recognise that Pareto's mechanical analogy only contends that the analytical instruments of rational mechanics provided useful analogies for both economics and sociology. There is no presumption that human conduct itself is mechanistic. In fact, the contrary is true, and was recognised by Pareto as such (with the distinction between logical and non-logical conduct introduced in recognition of complexities and vagaries of human conduct).

The outcome of this interpretative standpoint is an exposition of the complementary relationship between Pareto's pure economics and general sociology, which is relevant to the study of political conduct.

Samuels is similarly concerned with the relevance of Pareto's work for the study of political conduct. However, his interpretative standpoint is different, focusing on Pareto's sociological systems for the study of economic and social processes. Processes, history and dynamics are primary elements in Samuels' interpretative framework, which contrasts with my focus on statics as a consequence of the mechanical analogy. However, this must be seen in the context of Lausanne equilibrium analysis (as discussed in Section 5.1)

3.2. Formulation of Interpretative Stand Point

The interpretative formulation in *PES* derives from Vincent Tarascio's (1968) distinction between 'methodology' and 'method' in Pareto's work. That is, the distinction between the framework which defines the parameters of theory (i.e. the methodology) and the instruments or tools used to represent theory (i.e. the method). While the mechanical analogy primarily relates to the theoretical instruments that define Pareto's method, these economic and sociological theories, with respective emphasis on *homo œconomicus, interests, residues, derivations, elites*, are interpreted within their methodological context.

In regard to methodology, *PES* emphasises that, *inter alia*, specific concrete facts are understood through successive approximations. Under this approach, general regularities established within and between disciplines are synthetically united and in full recognition of 'interferences' between the regularities associated with various levels of approximation. In this context, general regularities established in pure or general theory largely concern the 'substantive' aspects of observable social conduct, with the 'form' that conduct takes being a secondary concern (although the form of conduct is important in Pareto's 'special' sociology and 'applied' economics).

In regard to method, the rapport between the elements of pure economics and general sociology is, consistent with Pareto's mechanical analogy, specified in a timeless manor. When movement is considered, it is in the context of 'virtual' change, thereby abstracting from the need to measure time. In this context, the level of generalised theoretical determinism is much broader and less precise when the conduct under investigation is non-logical than is the case when conduct is logical (as assumed in pure economics).

Samuels' interpretation does not assign prominence to Pareto's methodology (although he places considerable emphasis on the notion of 'logico-experimental knowledge') and he does not seek to formulate Pareto's contribution in terms of the relationship between pure economics and general sociology. Instead, he formulates the processes and dynamics of Paretian sociology. He does so in reference to three distinct social elements, namely (i) knowledge, (ii) psychology, and (iii) power,[1] and examines the interdependence between these elements, and the dynamic processes that emerge from this interaction.

On the face of it, the relative importance of dynamics and statics in Pareto's systems is given very different interpretation in our works.[2] However, the difference may not be as pronounced as it initially appears. As we agree that 'general' dynamic determinism is beyond the social sciences, our difference concerns how this should be dealt with. In *PES*, social theory is presented as 'timeless' to emphasise that Pareto's study of social equilibrium recognises that 'virtual' movements that would take (an unspecified amount of) time to complete.[3] Samuels, however, interprets Pareto's analysis of social movement as dynamic, but he recognises that the interdependence between power, knowledge and psychological dimensions of Pareto's social systems complicate analysis of the path of social change.

The fundamental difference between our approaches centres on the retention or abandonment of the equilibrium/disequilibrium system, with the different approaches to the role of time in theory being a second order issue.

3.3. Specification of Pareto's Evolving Ideas

PES captures the evolution of Pareto's ideas by surveying his major works. These include the 1896-97 *Cours d'Économie Politique* (Pareto, 1971); the 1901-02 *Les Systèmes Socialistes* (Pareto, 1974a); the 1906 *Manuale di Economia Politica* (Pareto, 1974b); and the 1916 *Trattato di Sociologia Generale* (Pareto, 1935), plus his major journal articles on methodology. The end result is an interpretation of Pareto inspired mainly by ideas raised by Pareto across his broad range of work prepared over many years.

Samuels, however, focuses almost exclusively on Pareto's most comprehensive mature work on social theory, the *Trattato*. As he did not set out to write a history of the development of Pareto's ideas, this cannot be criticised. Nevertheless, it does support the view that Samuels' interpretative framework is more influenced by specific aspects of Pareto's work than that revealed in the full range of Pareto's work. This is an important contributing factor to the originality of Samuels' reformulation and extension of Pareto's political sociology.

3.4. Choice of a Basis of Comparison

In regard to the mechanical analogy, the primary choice of comparison in *PES* was Phillip Mirowski's *More Heat than Light* (1989). This comparison established that, within Pareto's mechanical analogy, ophelimity is essentially economic utility subject to the constraint that utility fields are stable and independent of prior conduct (path-independent) when conduct is logical. In contrast, Pareto's concept of utility is generally used on the context where utility fields are unstable and path dependent when conduct is non-logical (i.e. utility, at a point in time, depends on prior conduct).

The second major comparison in *PES* is between the political sociology outlined in *Les Systèmes Socialistes* and James Buchanan's public choice/constitutional political economy. This establishes a certain similarity between the positive aspects Pareto's and Buchanan's work when sentiment is a stable, or at least constant, influence on conduct, and identifies major differences when sentiment is an unstable influence on political conduct. Pareto's approach is also used to highlight problems related to path-dependent utility fields for the normative aspects of constitutional political economy.

Samuels suggests that my interpretation may have been different if Pareto was compared to von Hayak instead of Buchanan. However, the influence of this comparison should not be overstated, as one of reason's for selecting Buchanan was to contrast his treatment of politics 'as exchange' with Pareto's treatment of the subject which focuses on power. Presumably, Samuels draws attention to this comparison because it identifies the circumstances when Buchanan's politics-as-exchange and Pareto's politics-as-power approaches are consistent, and when they are not. However, this result is, to a large degree, a consequence of earlier discussions on methodology (the distinction between form and substance) and the mechanical analogy (path-dependence of conduct inspired by sentiment).

In contrast, Samuels' work is more of a direct study of the *Tratatto* which does not rely on extensive comparisons with other authors.

4. REFORMULATION AND EXTENSION

The reformulation and extension of Pareto's political economy of public policy in *PES* is based on a distinction between two general categories of political conduct. The first category relates to the process of 'government', which refers to political decision-making and action undertaken with regard for the maintenance of, or acquisition of, political authority. The second category concerns 'public policy', which refers to political decision-making and action taken without regard for the maintenance of, or acquisition of, political authority.

4.1. Conformity, Residues and Preferences

These above-mentioned distinctions form the basis of a synthetic examination of politics via successive approximations. The first approximation explicitly focuses on the struggle for political authority. It considers substantial change in the level of conformity within the collective as well as change in the form of social organisation, (i.e. change without significant alteration to the level of conformity prevailing in the collective). The second approximation focuses on public policy, and more specifically, government initiated outcomes that may be represented as global or local variations within individuals' utility field.

In the *Trasformazione della democrazia*, Pareto notes that social influences that lead to erosion of uniformity and the consequent decentralisation of political authority are comparable to centrifugal forces (Pareto, 1984, 37). That is, an increase in non-conformist conduct within the collective reveals centrifugal force. Conversely, an increase in conformist conduct within the collective reveals centripetal force.

The framework advanced in *PES* classes 'substantial change' as a change in the degree of conformity prevailing in the collective bought about by actions of governing elites. Change in 'the form of the social collective' is associated with the conduct of ruling elites that need not have any impact on the degree of conformity prevailing in the collective.[4]

To consider the centralising and decentralising forces that act on the balance between conformist and non-conformist collectives, a range of preference types are developed in *PES* which derive from the relationship between Pareto's two main residues and utility. In view of this, it is first useful to recall that Pareto's notion of utility applies at two distinct levels[5] and in two distinct analytical contexts.

The two levels of utility, which are now quite common in welfare analysis, are referred to in this study as *personal utility* (benefit derived from one's own conduct) and *social utility* (benefit derived from the conduct of all members of the collective). The two analytical contexts concern (i) utility from the *extent of conformity of conduct* and (ii) utility from *economic goods* (i.e. as a function defined by commodity space). The first analytical context represents the most general relationship between people, conduct and utility, and is critical to consideration of the 'government' process. It concerns utility from the level of conformity in individual and collective conduct. The second form is consistent with the first, although it narrower and is a product of Pareto extending his analysis of collective economic maximisation (i.e. the first law of welfare economics) to encompass collective sociological maximisation, and is critical to consideration of the public policy process.[6]

There are four benchmark preference combinations that relate to utility experienced from the level of conformity of conduct, and account for individual's

Table 1. Preference Types Based on Individual's Personal Utility and Expected Social Utility

	Individual's Expected Social Utility is Maximised Under a **Conformist Collective**	Individual's Expected Social Utility is Maximised Under a **Non-conformist Collective**
Personality Residue Class I (**combinations**)	A type preferences	C type preferences
Personality Residue Class II (**preservation**)	B type preferences	D type preferences

personal utility and individual's *expected* social utility profiles, as shown in Table 1. These are incorporated within a Paretian 'elite' approach to political conduct, based on a patron-client model of political relations.

As is well known, Pareto illustrated his theory of elites with personality types variously referred to as lions, foxes, speculators and rentiers. The typical characterisation of Pareto's lions is given by B type preferences (individuals whose personal utility is maximised when their own conduct is conformist, and they also expect social utility to be maximised when conduct across the collective is generally conformist). The typical characterisation of Pareto's foxes and speculators is given by C type preferences (individuals whose personal utility is maximised when their conduct is non-conformist, and they also expect social utility to be maximised when conduct across the collective is also generally non-conformist).

However, individual preferences types are not uniquely related to lions of fox/speculators. For example, people who exhibit conduct associated with 'A type' preferences generally wish to live in conformist collectives. When living in a non-conformist social collective, they contribute to centralising or centripetal force for change. A type foxes emphasise indirect means to achieve substantial change and A type lions emphasise direct means. When A types are already elements of a conformist collective, they reveal preferences for a different form of the collective to that prevailing and/or a preference to maintain the existing social form and personally behave outside the norms of society.

4.2. The First Approximation – Government

In the case of a non-conformist collective, centralising centripetal forces are a force for 'substantial change', and the decentralising centrifugal forces constitute obstacles to this change. When a non-conformist collective has endured for some time, centralising force is associated with A type preferences and the opposing centrifugal force is represented by the existing elite with D type preferences. If the non-conformist collective has not endured for long, then the

Table 2. Forces For, and Obstacles To, Substantial Change in Government Activity

Type of Collective	Force for Change	Obstacles to Change
Conformist: established elite	Centrifugal: C type preferences	Centripetal: B type preferences
Conformist: new elite	Centrifugal: D type preferences	Centripetal: A type preferences
Non-conformist: established elite	Centripetal: A type preferences	Centrifugal: D type preferences
Non-conformist: new elite	Centripetal: B type preferences	Centrifugal: C type preferences

centripetal force for substantial change is associated with B type preferences, that is, by elements rich in Class II residues who seek to return society to the patriotic and conformist days of the recent past. The opposing centrifugal forces are associated C type preferences, the moderns of the new elite.

In the case of a conformist collective, the reverse applies. Centralising centripetal forces are an obstacle to 'substantial change', and decentralising centrifugal forces constitute a force for change. If the conformist collective has endured for some time, the centripetal force is associated with B type preferences and is an obstacle to change. In this case the opposing centrifugal force is represented by a potential new elite rich in C type preferences and is a force for change. If the conformist collective has not endured for long, then the centrifugal force of D type preferences and is a force for change. That is, elements rich in Class II residues seek to return society to the freedom and non-conformist days of the recent past. The opposing centripetal force is associated with fox/speculators and lions with A preferences, the moderns of the new elite.

The justification for this 'preference type' approach is clear. If one equates speculator/foxes with C type preferences and lions with B type preference, substantial change in (i) an established non-conformist collective or (ii) a conformist collective with a new elite, cannot be well explained by speculator/foxes and lions alone. A type and D type preferences also needed when clarifying the balance between the forces of centralisation and decentralisation. This also has implications for Samuels' analysis, as discussed in Section 5.

Just as governing elites employ derivations that draw on the imagery of substantive change to justify their achievements, alternative governing elites use derivations to highlight the substantive improvements they will make in office. However, the extent of the substantive change in collective conformity is often less significant than the associated derivations suggest. In stable political systems, change largely concerns the form of government (such as the replacement of one incumbent government by another, while the constitutional arrangements for political selection endure), or only a moderate incremental change in the degree of collective conformity.

When a collective is relatively conformist, only A type preferences constitute a force for change in the social or political form. This is because the forces for local change are limited to individuals who support the substantive level of conformity prevailing in the collective, but as they are rich in Class I residues, a preference for a change in the social form may be implied. The countervailing conservative force in this context is the conduct of people with B types preferences.

When a collective is relatively non-conformist, only C type preferences constitute a force for change in the social or political form. Forces for change are limited to elements that support the substantive level of non-conformist conduct prevailing in the collective, but as they are rich in Class I residues, a preference for a change in the social form may be implied. The countervailing conservative force in this context is the conduct of people with D types preferences.

4.3. The Second Approximation – Public Policy

If theory is to provide 'positive' foundations for the study of 'public policy', then there must be a basis for the subjective intent of policy to agree with its objective purpose. This would ensure that the expected change in utility (whether it is represented as a quantity or a variation between ordinal index numbers) is realised, thereby eliminating ongoing revision to the desired end of policy when logically implemented.

From the earlier discussion, there can be little doubt that the limits of a positive approach to policy are severe for the first approximation of the political conduct. However, this does not extend to the second approximation, where, subject to stable balance of power under the first approximation, the process of public policy can be considered in isolation from the struggle for political authority. This can be considered at the 'global' and 'local' level.

Global policy is considered in the context of any potential variations to individuals' position in their utility field (defined in commodity space) following public intervention. When implementing global policy, governments act logically by recognising that human conduct is predominantly non-logical, and within this constraint, attempting to maximise the level of social utility. In this context, policy itself is 'scientific' or positive to the extent that it recognises the instability of non-logical preferences, and uses political authority to stabilise general perceptions of collective welfare.

In terms of pure theory, Pareto's approach to collective economic and sociological maximisation is generally discussed on a global basis. However, in relation to public policy, the dominance of non-logical over logical conduct largely confines the relevant scope of the Pareto's principle (where unequivocal gain requires at least one person to gain and no one to be worse off) to local variations in commodity space. The approach to sociological maxima when this principle is abandoned, as outlined in Pareto's "Il Massimo di utilità per una collectività in sociologia" (Pareto, 1980b), facilitates consideration of welfare matters for more substantive variations in commodity space.

To the extent that public policy does not reflect the goal of maximising social welfare, the global policy process is non-logical. This reflects a judgement that policy processes that deviate from this goal are path dependent. However, non-logical aspects of public policy may also reflect institutional arrangements – such as fora for voting, parliaments etc. – which may also be analysed within Buchanan's public choice tradition. This would complement the Paretian analysis proposed in *PES*. It may also provide an indication of when political conduct, which superficially appears to be independent of the struggle for political authority, should also be considered using the broader 'government level' analysis.

Local policy involves small variations in individual's commodity space as a consequence of public intervention. It can also be logical or non-logical.

When the subjective purpose of local policy is to improve social utility, this may be achieved by a sub-global application of the Pareto principle. For example, reduction of compliance costs for taxpayers, or reducing the cost of service provision. Local policy would also be logical if the incidence of 'losers' is consistent with the political welfare function of the logical global policy framework. Public choice techniques can also be used to diagnose whether this type of policy is logical in a Paretian welfare sense, or whether the self-interest of public administrators dominates under given institutional arrangements.

5. THE EQUILIBRIUM APPROACH – A SOURCE OF DISCOMFORT?

As noted in section one, Samuels' discomfort with the reformulation and extension in *PES* concerns the prominent role assigned to equilibrium. The issues of particular concern are the reduced 'openendedness' of the system, the use of a narrower definition of positive theory than the broadest adopted by Pareto and the particular application of ideas developed in *Pareto on Policy* within an equilibrium context in *PES*. It is useful to preface my response to these particular concerns with some observations on Pareto's Walrasian heritage on the issue of equilibrium and time.

5.1. Equilibrium and Time – Pareto's Walrasian Heritage

While the difference between Walras and Pareto on the methodology of social science is too great to be reconciled, there is little doubt that Walras' system of general equilibrium is the single most important intellectual influence on Pareto the theorist. The defining feature of the Lausanne School's contribution to the social sciences is its focus on equilibrium, and its attempts to develop an equilibrium approach that was a genuine approximation to dynamic behaviour. The dynamic issues considered in the *Trattato*, which are of such interest to Samuels, are not independent of Walras work on equilibrium. When the relationship between time and equilibrium in the work of the Lausanne School is considered, the *prima facie* contrast between Samuels and myself on Pareto becomes less distinct.

The modern conception of Walrasian general equilibrium has several major differences to the Walras' own work. Maks and van Daal (forthcoming) suggest that almost all textbooks present Walrasian equilibrium along the lines of studies undertaken in the mid-twentieth century by Arrow and Debreu on the existence of a unique point of general equilibrium. As such, the modern general appreciation of Walras focuses on exchange and production, setting Walras' treatment on savings, money and capital formation aside, and on the conditions for equilibrium, setting aside – or treating in a very trivial manner – Walras' examination of movement towards equilibrium in a period and the dynamic attributes of movement between periods.

Based on Maks and van Daal (forthcoming) assessment of Walras, it can be argued that Walras regarded equilibrium in a period as efficient, but the *tâtonnement* or the within-period endogenous movement towards equilibrium are not a strictly logical process (at least not in the Paretian sense). Furthermore, when movement is considered as a sequence of 'between period' equilibria, Walras did not theorise about inter-period equilibrium as he recognised that changes in preferences and the quantity and quality of the capital stock are unlikely to be co-ordinated over time, thereby preventing the achievement of inter-temporal efficiency – strict rational expectations are not assumed.

Pareto's initial response to these issues was to largely remove *tâtonnement* from pure theory of economics and treat movements to equilibrium, both in a period and between periods, as part of a general cyclical theory of social equilibrium outlined in the *Cours*, which was presented as a part of 'applied economics'. Pareto subsequently took the subject of social equilibrium out of applied economics and made it the 'centre piece' of a new theory, namely general sociology. In this general theoretical context, when Pareto considered broad movements around a stable social equilibrium, he was effectively working in a theoretical space that is similar to Walras' analysis of within period movements to equilibrium through *tâtonnement.* As such, the potential for a positive foundation of policy exists, as long as it is recognised that such movements take time to complete (which involves periods of minor disequilibrium). In contrast, when Pareto examined unstable social equilibrium, he was effectively working in a theoretical space that is similar to Walras' treatment of between period equilibria. While particular forces for change can be identified, the change remains opendended and there is no basis for making welfare assessments between social states under different social equilibria.

The important point is that the different contexts of equilibrium (stable/unstable, within period/between period, economic/sociological) provided the theoretical mechanism by which the Lausanne School accounted for the various circumstances when the impact of time has greater or lesser influence on human conduct. Focusing on the dynamic aspects of Pareto's work without considering the equilibrium context in which these observations were derived yields a partial picture. In large part, it would appear that the different approaches to dynamics and time in *PES* and *Pareto on Policy* are not as great as Samuels suggests, at least not once it is recognised that the dynamic issues that Samuels regards as outside the scope of the equilibrium approach where generally accommodated within an equilibrium framework by both masters of the Lausanne School.

5.2. Reduced Openendedess

Samuels points out that the approach developed in *PES* reduces the openendedness of Pareto's total system. To some extent, this is correct. Nevertheless, as utility is usually considered in the context of path-dependent conduct, where individuals' expected variation in social utility from substantial social change is unlikely to be realised, only modest reductions have been achieved. In this regard, the 'first approximation' outlined in *PES* can either: verify the existence of a stable social equilibrium (i.e. balance of power at a constant level of conformism/non-conformism in society); or when the equilibrium is found to be unstable:

- establish the direction of forces for substantive social change (i.e. an increase or decrease in the level of conformist conduct within the collective); or
- establish whether change is largely confined to the 'form' of society.

It cannot establish whether a new point of social equilibrium will be stable or unstable, or provide much certainty about the extent of likely changes in the substantive or formal aspects of society. The analytical system can only be closed when the current social equilibrium is stable and public policy, as considered in the 'second approximation', is undertaken on a logical basis.

5.3. 'Positive' Science of Policy

Samuels' comments on a narrower 'positive theory of public policy' are particularly interesting, as they are also related to 'openendedness' of Pareto's work.

The issue of positive science of policy was raised in *PES* because there were two opposite views on the matter in the literature.[7] Tarascio was of the view that Pareto's contribution to a positive policy is overlooked (Tarascio, 1968, 55), especially his 1913 "Il Massimo di utilità per una collectività in sociologia" (Pareto, 1980b). Busino, however, rejected Tarascio's proposition with the observation that Pareto thought it practically impossible to elaborate a positive policy (Busino, 1974, 223).

PES demonstrates that, at the level of the first approximation, we cannot determine, on an *a-priori* basis, whether the change in either the form or substance of society enhances collective welfare (unless change marks a reduction in extreme levels of conformist or non-conformist conduct).[8] Furthermore, we cannot determine the precise point at which forces for social change will find a new stable social equilibrium when the prevailing social equilibrium is unstable. As social movement itself will modify the relationship between individuals' well being and the conduct of members of the collective (i.e. utility is path-dependent), such precision is beyond the scope of analytical tools within an equilibrium framework.

In contrast, the goal of maximising social utility at the level of the second approximation can, when the first approximation indicates that the social equilibrium is stable, be realised by the ruling elite imposing some stability on individuals' expected social utility, thereby creating a stable social utility function. This allows government policy decisions to be treated as if they are the result of a 'logical' process aimed at maximising social utility.

From this we may conclude that Busino is correct to the extent that there are overwhelming obstacles to a positive study of the process of government. However, when the struggle for political power is balanced because social equilibrium is stable, Pareto's work contributes significantly to a positive theory of public policy (as Tarascio affirms).

Samuels raises the definition of positive policy, not to contest the above result, but to indicate that some of Pareto's work implies a broader positive framework. In this regard, policy developed from 'logico-experimental' knowledge gives the policy maker the capacity to understand the psychology of the governed, and the capacity to manipulate preferences to achieve their ends. The difference between Samuels and the Tarascio/Busino/*PES* discussion of positive policy is that the former does not limit the phrase to conduct in pursuit of welfare maximising policy goals, whereas the latter do. As Pareto discussed both contexts (and indeed while he regarded welfare maximising public policy as logical, he acknowledged it was the exception rather than the rule), Samuels comment on this matter is valid.

5.4. Use of Pareto on Policy

Samuels expresses some discomfort with the application of his ideas in *PES*. The other side of this is my comfort with the ideas expressed in *Pareto on Policy*. Notwithstanding the mixed initial reaction to *Pareto on Policy* (with Tarascio (1975) reviewing it unfavourably and Backhaus (1977) reviewing it positively), it is an important and original study. In the form that it is presented, with the emphasis on processes and institutions and incremental change, it takes Pareto's *general sociology*, and prepares it for application as a *special sociology*. That is, *Pareto on Policy* provides the analyst with a guide to study incremental change, at a specific point in time and under given institutional arrangements, due to interdependencies. It also distinguishes between analysis of collective decision making and the use of that analysis to generate policy, including preferred policy. *PES*, in contrast, is more abstract, and deals with regularities of elite conduct. As such, it remains closer to a 'general' sociology, but integrated with economics through successive approximations. Although different, *PES* is nevertheless complemented by Samuels' work, in much the same way that Pareto envisaged 'special' sociology would complement 'general' sociology.

As noted in Section 3, *Pareto on Policy* examines the positive groundwork in Pareto's *Trattato* for the study of political processes by emphasising general interdependence between 'three' elements of political conduct, namely (i) knowledge, (ii) psychology, and (iii) power.[9] It also employs two measures to consider the political process. One is the continuum between the extremes of freedom and authority. The second is the continuum between the extremes of continuity and change. The former refers to the degree of control that the governing elite exercises over the subject classes, whereas the latter measures the degree of social change consequent upon decision-making.

When considered in isolation, the 'knowledge' dimension provides the general context of the policy framework, the 'psychology' dimension relates to continuity and change and the 'power' dimension relates to freedom and control. However, this oversimplifies Samuels' interpretation because he explicitly accounts for Paretian interdependencies. Actions are not only manifestations of psychic states, they also reveal preferences concerning social states, including individuals' propensity to manipulate by means of force or cunning. As a result, knowledge, psychology and power are inter-related through residues. Persuasion is related to beliefs that accord with sentiments that are objectively observed as residues. As a result, knowledge, psychology and power are all inter-related through derivations as well, but the constant element of derivations is the sentiments they reflect. In all instances, the interdependencies have a basic source – the human psyche – but the interdependencies between each element nevertheless impact on social equilibrium.

This also has the effect of blurring the distinction between the freedom/control continuum and the continuity/change continuum. In view of this, Samuels contended that matters related to freedom and control can be specified in terms of continuity and change. Conversely, continuity and change can be considered in terms of freedom and control matters (Samuels, 1974, 154).

The above relationship is the starting point for the first approximation to politics developed in *PES*, with government processes discussed in terms of continuity and change, and related to freedom and control. Samuels' discomfort derives from the application of his notions in an equilibrium framework where government and policy activities are differentiated.

Nevertheless, incorporating Samuels' analysis in *PES* yields two worthwhile results. First, it shows that, when considering the question of 'substantial' change in social equilibrium due to an adjustment in the balance of power, the formulation does not hold. That is, direct force (control) is not uniquely associated with continuity and freedom does not necessarily correspond with substantial change. Second, when a change in form is considered, Samuels formulation holds when it is assumed that directly confrontationist behaviour is confined to individuals rich in Class II residues and indirect non-confrontationist behaviour is limited to individuals rich in Class I residues.

6. CONCLUSION – THE RELEVANCE OF PARETO

At an early stage in his distinguished career, Giovanni Busino noted that:

> Celebrated economists and famous sociologists have spoken of Vilfredo Pareto with such science and penetration that it is very difficult to add anything that is not stale repetition. (Busino, 1964)

Variations in modern interpretations of Pareto can largely be explained by differences in interpretive frameworks, as demonstrated in the case of Samuels and *PES* in Section 3 of this paper. Nevertheless, such variations are important, as they constitute the foundations for work that extends and enhances aspects of Pareto's work.

Even a casual reading of *Pareto on Policy* and *PES* suggests that Samuels and I share the view that the current relevance of Pareto to modern political economy centres on an expanded role for Pareto's political sociology. Foremost in this regard is the relationship between elements of the social system, the dominant role of elites in the struggle for political authority and in the policy development process, and the prominence of non-logical conduct within the collective. We disagree on whether this should be achieved by building a bridge between political sociology and general equilibrium economics, or as something distinct from modern economics. In other words, while we are in accord on the 'substantive' issue (that Pareto's political sociology is relevant to modern political economy), we are not in accord on the 'form' in which modern political economy should be expressed. The two approaches are therefore complementary. Furthermore, a full reconciliation of the approaches could be achieved, if desired, by examining the interdependencies between power, knowledge and psychology to consider the path of 'between period' social change and adopting the equilibrium-efficiency approach when social movement is considered from an initial given social state, including preferences, elites and non-logical conduct, especially when the in-period equilibrium is stable.

Interestingly, the substantive aspects of Pareto's political sociology noted above readily fall within the scope of heterodox approaches to political economy. However, in view of the ongoing association of Pareto with optmisation and equilibrium, I suspect that most heterodox political economists are unlikely to investigate Pareto's political sociology or incorporate it within their studies. Even Samuels' study of Pareto's political sociology was more successful in attracting the interest of historians of economic thought and Paretian specialists than that of institutionalists or heterodox political economists.

Contemporary orthodox economists have not shown much more interest in accommodating Pareto's political sociology within economics than their heterodox colleagues, even though the potential to do so is significant (as highlighted in *PES*). One obvious example is the scope for the public choice economics to complement Pareto's general regularity approach to politics.[10] However, again, the main interest within the English-speaking world in the relationship between economics and sociology comes from historians of economic thought, most notably Vincent Tarascio.

This may lead one to speculate that, in regard to contemporary economists, Pareto's total system is considered too orthodox by the heterodox and too heterodox by the orthodox. One could even reach a similar conclusion in regard to Walras, as his treatment of time and social economics is not well appreciated by orthodox economists and his equilibrium economics is not of major interest to heterodox economists. However, this case should not be stated to strongly as it is the product of oversimplification. Pareto, if nothing else, caused perspectives to alter. When other theorists were examining capital and labour relations, Pareto was also examining the relationship between speculators and rentiers. When other theorists were talking about the struggle between socialists and fascists, Pareto was also examining the balance between the individual and the collective. Pareto was an innovative and challenging multidisciplinary theorist. He was never far from controversy, and his work remains too complex and broad in scope to be accurately labelled in terms of the orthodox or heterodox dicotomy.[11]

While Pareto's multidisciplinary methodology and his political sociology have never been at the forefront of critical developments in English language political economy, the relevance of Pareto's sociology to many developments in political economy has been pointed out at various intervals throughout the 20th Century. For example, the social welfare function (Bergson, 1938, 1983; Tarascio, 1968, 1993; Chipman, 1976), public choice theory (Backhaus, 1978; Maneschi, 1993), public finance (Fasiani, 1949; Tarascio, 1974), merit goods (McLure, 2001), evolutionary theory (Houghton and Lopreato, 1977), cycles and macroeconomics (Tarascio, 1969; Powers, 1984) and public policy generally (Samuels, 1974; Tarascio, 1975).

My judgement is that Pareto's single greatest insight into the social sciences is his (anti Walrasian) multidisciplinary methodology, including his distinction between substance and form, and general and special studies. However, as the economics profession does not generally appreciate the subtleties of Pareto's methodology (as it is either ignored or considered in a superficial manner),[12] the probability of Pareto now having a major influence on modern political economy is low. The profession has simply taken a very different path to that advocated by Pareto, with the scope and application of axiomatic models of rational conduct becoming more circumstance specific and ever expanding, rather than carefully examining and limiting the scope of pure economic theory as a general system of analysis. Consider for example the development of axiomatic social welfare theory as well as game theory and the consequent application of the rational hypothesis at many stages of economic processes and public policy.

While modern political economy will not be radically rewritten due to a revival of Paretian political sociology, in the last ten years several major works have emerged which shed considerable light on Pareto's political sociology, some of which may come to influence political economy. Examples include: *Pareto Oggi* (Busino, 1991), *La Ragione e i Sentimenti* (Rutigliano, 1994), *La Sociologia di Vilfredo Pareto e il Senso della Modernità* (Maniscalco, 1994) and "L'Équilibre Général: Entre économie at sociologie" (Bridel and Tatti, 1999). Fiorenzo Mornati (formerly of the Walras-Pareto Centre at the University of Lausanne) is also currently engaged in a very substantial Paretian research program, the results of which will be published in the next few years.

The language in which the above studies are written clearly demonstrates that Europe (mainly Italy) is the dominant centre of Paretian studies. It is my hope that these European studies, and my own *PES*, will be influential to the extent that modern political economy searches for explanations that place diminish reliance on axiomatic models of rational economic actors.

NOTES

1. Samuels individually relates these to a range of Paretian concepts associated with the internal elements of social equilibrium. The 'knowledge' dimension incorporates the Paretian treatment of logico-experimental and non-logico-experimental knowledge, derivations, and utility of the social system. The 'psychology' dimension refers to sentiment and residues, and their correlations with speculator and rentier conduct, their impact on governing elites, and the consequence for social equilibrium. The 'power' dimension refers to the circulation of elites and social heterogeneity, the associated issues of the ruling class (i.e. the governing elite and the alternative governing elites), and manipulation by force and cunning.
2. Interestingly, this has been a long running difficulty in interpreting the role of time in Pareto's sociological systems. For example, Werner Stark's assessment is that Pareto's sociology is "blinded by the timelessness and universality of mechanical regularities" (Stark, 1965, p. 54). While endorsing the mechanistic interpretation of Pareto's body of work, Stark regarding it as a backward step in the development of the social sciences. In contrast, Joseph Lopreato emphasises that Pareto "... indissolubly joined sociology with history and above all founded sociology on history" (Lopreato, 1973, p. 456). John Houghton and Joseph Lopreato subsequently noted that "Pareto is often falsely accused of basing his sociology on 'physicalistic' or 'mechanistic' analogies" (Houghton and Lopreato, 1977, p. 19), when his ultimate goal was "an evolutionary social science" (Houghton and Lopreato, 1977, p. 20). These different interpretations are largely due to Pareto's use of a methodology which, in Stark's phrase, emphasises 'timelessness and universalism', while at the same time, complementing this timeless analysis with extensive reference to historical information and induction which suggests an ordering of events.
3. This can be justified by Pareto's contention that the existence of economic and social cycles, and the forces that contribute to these cyclical movements is a more fundamental theoretical concern than determining a dynamic processes (which is more concerned with the 'form' of social organisation than it is with its 'substance').
4. For example, substantial change is most probable following a change in centripetal and centrifugal forces such as social upheaval or a violent change in government that results in a change in the level of state control over social arrangements. A movement from an essentially individualistic system to a socialist system in response to centripetal force constitutes a substantial change. In contrast, a change in the form of political conduct is likely to be associated with the election of a new government in a stable parliamentary system of government. Similarly, a change from a popular or worker's socialist government to a capitalist's socialist system would constitute a change in the 'form' of the collective if the level of state control in the collective was unchanged.
5. A third distinct level of utility is mentioned in the *Cours*, 'utility of the species' (Pareto, 1971, p. 1086), but was not subsequently developed by Pareto and is not considered here.
6. This has its basis in Pareto's now famous 1913 article *Il Massimo di utilità per una collectività in sociologia* (Pareto, 1980b), and in the subsequent discussion of the issue in the *Trattato* (1935, p. 1470-4). In these works, Pareto restates his conclusions on the maximisation of collective economic welfare, and extends them to sociological maximisation using a two-stage process for converting utility into homogeneous quantities. The resultant weighting by each individual of their own welfare together with other individuals' welfare, followed by government's weighting of these individual weightings has been called the 'political welfare function' (Tarascio, 1993, p. 52).

7. The phrase 'positive theory of policy' is used here in the context of a 'scientific' approach to policy. It should not be confused with the philosophy of logical positivism, or the positivists who were contemporaries of Pareto (who Pareto regarded as largely rationalising outcomes).
8. Extreme non-conformist or extreme conformist collective social orders do not accommodate conduct of the various general classes of residues, implying potential gains in utility from change to less extreme forms of social order. Hence, "In an environment imbued with authoritarian principles, a religion of free will can be useful; in an environment tending to anarchy an authoritarian religion is indispensable if the dissolution of society is to be impeded. On the other hand, it is of little importance if the form of this religion is new or ancient" (Pareto, 1980a, p. 323).
9. As discussed in Section 3 and note 1 above.
10. Similarities between Pareto and public choice are also examined in Backhouse (1978).
11. Busino (1974, p. 224) made a similar point when reviewing Tarascio (1968).
12. There are, of course, some notable and important exceptions such as Schumpeter (1949), Alais (1968) and Tarascio (1968, 1993, 1999).

REFERENCES

Allais, M. (1968). "Pareto, Vilfredo: Contributions to Economics", *Encyclopedia of the Social Sciences*, New York, Macmillan, Vol. II, 399-411.

Backhaus, J. (1977). "Towards an Integrated Theory of Social Systems", *American Journal of Economics and Sociology*, Vol. 36, No. 2, 217-223.

Backhaus, J. (1978). "Pareto on Public Choice", *Public Choice,* Vol. 33, No. 1, 5-17, reproduced in John Wood and Michael McLure (eds.), 1999, *Vilfredo Pareto: Critical Assessments*, Vol. 4, London, Routledge, 395-407.

Bergson, A. (1938). "A Reformation of Certain Aspects of Welfare Economics", *Quarterly Journal of Economics*, Vol. 52, 3-26, reproduced in John Wood and Michael McLure (eds.), 1999, *Vilfredo Pareto: Critical Assessments*, Vol. 2, Routledge, London, 297-316.

Bergson, A. (1983). "Pareto on Social Welfare", *Journal of Economic Literature*, Vol. 21, No. 1, 40-60, reproduced in John Wood and Michael McLure (eds.), 1999, *Vilfredo Pareto: Critical Assessments*, Vol. 3, London, Routledge, 348-357.

Bridel, P. and Tatti, E. (eds.) (1999). "L'Équilibre Général: Entre économie at sociologie", *Revue Européene des Sciences Sociales,* Vol. 37, No. 116, 1-380.

Busino, G. (1964). "In Margine dell'Edizione dell' «Opera Omnia»", *Rassegna economica*, May-August, pp. 3-12, reproduced in Busino, G. (1974), *Gli Studi su Vilfredo Pareto Oggi*, Roma, Bulzoni Editore, 15-29.

Busino, G. (1974). *Gli Studi su Vilfredo Pareto Oggi*, Roma, Bulzoni Editore.

Busino, G. (ed.) (1991). *Pareto Oggi*, Bologna, il Mulino.

Chipman, J. (1976). "The Paretian Heritage", *Revue Européene des Sciences Sociales,* No. 37, 65-173, reproduced in John Wood and Michael McLure (eds.), 1999, *Vilfredo Pareto: Critical Assessments*, Vol. 2, London, Routledge, 157-257.

Fasiani, M. (1949). "Contributi di Pareto alla Scienza delle Finanze", *Vilfredo Pareto: L'economista e il Sociologo*, Università Commerciale "Luigi Boconi", Milano, Casa Editrice Rodolfo Malfasi, 263-307.

Houghton, J. and Lopreato, J. (1977). "Towards a Theory of Social Evolution: The Paretian Groundwork", *Revue Européene des Sciences Sociales,* Vol. 15, No. 40, 19-38, reproduced in

John Wood and Michael McLure (eds.), 1999, *Vilfredo Pareto: Critical Assessments*, Vol. 3, London, Routledge, 95-114.

Lopreato, J. (1973). "Notes on the Work of Vilfredo Pareto", *Social Science Quarterly*, Vol. 54, No. 3, 451-68, reproduced in John Wood and Michael McLure (eds.) 1999, *Vilfredo Pareto: Critical Assessments*, Vol. 1, London, Routledge, 328-45.

Maks, J.A.H. and van Daal, J. (forthcoming). "Léon Walras: What Cutes Know and What They Should Know", in *Founders of Modern Economics*, Backhaus, J. (ed.), Cheltenham, Edward Elgar.

Maneschi, A. (1993). "Pareto on International Trade Theory and Policy", *Journal of the History of Economic Thought*, Vol. 15, Fall, 210-228, reproduced in John Wood and Michael McLure (eds.), 1999, *Vilfredo Pareto: Critical Assessments*, Vol. 4, London, Routledge, 422-437.

Maniscalco, M.L. (1994). *La Sociologia di Vilfredo Pareto e il Senso della Modernità*, Milano, FrancoAngeli.

McLure, M. (2001). *Pareto Economics and Society: The Mechanical Analogy*, London, Routledge.

Mirowski, P. (1989). *More Heat Than Light. Economics as Social Physics: Physics as Nature's Economics*, Cambridge, Cambridge University Press.

Pareto, V. (1935) [1916]. *The Mind and Society [Trattato di Sociologia Generale]*, New York, Harcourt, Brace and Company.

Pareto, V. (1971) [1896-97]. *Corso di Economia Politica [Cours d'Économie Politique]*, Torino, Unione Tipographico-Editrice Torinese.

Pareto, V. (1974a) [1901-02]. *I Sistemi Socialisti [Les Systèmes Socialistes]*, Torino: Unione Tipografico-Editrice Torinese.

Pareto, V. (1974b) [1906]. *Manuale di Economia Politica con una Introduzione alla Scienza Sociale*, Padova, Casa Editrice Dott. Antonio Milani.

Pareto, V. (1980a) [1907]. "La Questione Religiosa", *Ouvres Complètes, Tome XXII, Écrites sociologiques mineurs*, ed. G. Busino, Genéve, Librairie Droz, 322-323.

Pareto, V. (1980b) [1913]. "Il Massimo di Utilità per una Collettività in Sociologia", *Ouvres Complètes, Tome XXII, Écrites sociologiques mineurs*, ed. G. Busino, Genéve, Librairie Droz, 601-605, reproduced under the title *The Community's Utility Maximum in Sociology* in John Wood and Michael McLure (eds.), 1999, *Vilfredo Pareto: Critical Assessments*, Vol. 3, London, Routledge, 307-10.

Pareto, V. (1984) [1921]. *The Transformation of Democracy [Trasformazione della Democrazia]*, New Brunswick, Transaction Books.

Powers, C. (1984). "Socio Political Determinants of Economic Cycles: Vilfredo Pareto's Final Statement", *Social Science Quarterly*, Vol. 65, No. 4, 988-1001.

Rutigliano, E. (ed.) (1994). *La Ragione e i Sentimenti: Vilfredo Pareto e la Sociologia*, Milano, FrancoAngeli.

Samuels, W.J. (1974). *Pareto on Policy*, Amsterdam, Elsevier Scientific Publishing Company.

Samuels, W.J. (2001). "Introduction", in *Pareto Economics and Society: The Mechanical Analogy*, Michael McLure, London, Routledge.

Schumpeter, J.A. (1949). "Vilfredo Pareto (1848-1923)", *Quarterly Journal of Economics*, Vol. 63, May, 147-173, reproduced in John Wood and Michael McLure (eds.), 1999, *Vilfredo Pareto: Critical Assessments*, Vol. 1, London, Routledge, 106-28.

Stark, W. (1965) [1963]. "In Search of the True Pareto", in *Pareto and Mosca*, J. Meisel (ed.), Englewood Cliffs, Prentice Hall, 45-55.

Tarascio, V.J. (1968). *Pareto's Methodological Approach to Economics*, Chapel Hill, University of North Carolina Press.

Tarascio, V.J. (1969). "The Monetary and Employment Theories of Vilfredo Pareto", *History of Political Economy*, Vol. 6, No. 4, 361-80.

Tarascio, V.J. (1974). "Pareto on Political Economy", *History of Political Economy,* Vol. 6, No. 4, 361-380, reproduced in John Wood and Michael McLure (eds.), 1999, *Vilfredo Pareto: Critical Assessments*, Vol. 3, London, Routledge, 330-347.

Tarascio, V.J. (1975). "Pareto on Policy. By Warren J. Samuels", *Journal of Political Economy*, Vol. 83, No. 4, 880-2.

Tarascio, V.J. (1993). "Pareto's Sociological Model of Man", *History of Economics Review,* Vol. 19, pp. 49-54, reproduced in John Wood and Michael McLure (eds.), 1999, *Vilfredo Pareto: Critical Assessments*, Vol. 3, London, Routledge, 376-83.

Tarascio, V. J. (1999). "The Problem of Scope: Walras and Pareto", *Revue Européene des Sciences Sociales,* Vol. 36, No. 16, 295-314.